Problem-Based
Learning

in Middle and High School Classrooms

To my father, John Lambros,
and in loving memory of my mother, Dorothy Lambros,
who taught me that no matter what else changes,
our family is always steadfast.
And to my sister Debbie,
who loves me through the best and worst of times.
I am eternally grateful that she is part of my life.

Problem-Based **Learning**

in Middle and High School Classrooms

A Teacher's Guide to Implementation

Ann Lambros

CORWIN PRESS
A Sage Publications Company
Thousand Oaks, California

For information:

Corwin Press
A Sage Publications Company
2455 Teller Road
Thousand Oaks, California 91320
www.corwinpress.com

Sage Publications Ltd.
1 Oliver's Yard
55 City Road
London EC1Y 1SP
United Kingdom

Sage Publications India Pvt. Ltd.
B-42, Panchsheel Enclave
Post Box 4109
New Delhi 110 017 India

Printed in the United States of America

Library of Congress Cataloging-in-Publication Data

Lambros, Ann.
Problem-based learning in middle and high school classrooms: A teacher's guide to implementation / by Ann Lambros.
    p. cm.
Includes bibliographical references and index.
ISBN 0-7619-3846-X (cloth) — ISBN 0-7619-3847-8 (paper)
    1. Problem-based learning. 2. Problem-solving—Study and teaching (Secondary) I. Title.
LB1027.42.K37 2004
371.39—dc22   2003023411

This book is printed on acid-free paper.

04   05   06   07   10   9   8   7   6   5   4   3   2   1

Acquisitions Editor:	Faye Zucker
Editorial Assistant:	Stacy Wagner
Production Editor:	Denise Santoyo
Copy Editor:	Barbara Coster
Typesetter:	C&M Digitals (P) Ltd.
Indexer:	Pamela Van Huss
Cover Designer:	Michael Dubowe

Contents

Preface

Preparing middle school students for high school and high school students for what awaits them after graduation presents a host of challenges long recognized by teachers, parents, and administrators. There are issues around academic development, noncognitive skills development, and social maturity development. Now add issues of career choice, information bombardment, and newly experienced expectations from teachers and parents. It is of little wonder that so much is written about strategies to manage these school and life transitions for middle and high school students. The categories seem almost as endless as the issues themselves. There are the transitions from elementary to middle school, from middle school to high school, from high school to college, from high school to the world of work or from high school to the widest ever range of postsecondary educational opportunities. There are online education, distance education, and virtual classrooms in addition to the more traditional community college or 4-year university setting.

Students today need a set of skills not only for managing these transitions but for decision making, problem solving, and self-direction as they have never needed them before this century. It is a seemingly full-time proposition to prepare students with a skill set just to meet these kinds of demands. Yet, in today's accountability-driven culture, there is hardly time to address the basic issues of content coverage and curricular objectives. How can a teacher feel that the instruction provided can adequately address content issues, process issues, and social development issues?

Let's first consider the dilemmas faced by many high school students as they graduate. Too many students leave high school without the skills to succeed in the workplace or in postsecondary institutions. These students will, sadly, find themselves unprepared for the rigor of college courses, the expectations of employers, and the need to self-direct a significant portion of their learning, whether on the job or in the classroom.

In an article titled "Ticket to Nowhere" (Haycock, 1999), the state of unpreparedness among high school graduates is underscored: "Currently about three-quarters of high school graduates will go to college within two years of graduation. If present growth rates continue, more than 80% of today's sixth graders will end up in college. But unless the secondary school experience of these young sixth graders differs radically from that of the students who preceded them, many of them will arrive utterly unprepared for college-level work and will spend their first year or more taking high school level courses." This unfortunate prediction may have even more serious implications for students who arrive at colleges and universities with innovative courses and programs such as problem-based learning and who have had no experience with this or similar challenging methodologies.

Likewise, middle school students who have either just arrived at middle school or are nearer to the high school transition often find themselves ill equipped for the new challenges they are facing. Their academic course work is more demanding than their previous experiences in elementary school, they are required to work more independently than ever, and they are faced with more choices. At the same time, their physical and social development is occurring at its most accelerated rate, and friends have become a significant influence in decision-making processes. Unfortunately, these students are rarely skilled at decision making, determining best choices, or working in collaboration with peers who may not be in their circle of friends. Middle school students have usually not developed a process for dealing with so many shifts and demands because it has not been necessary to do so.

What to Do? Why to Do It?

Problem-based learning (PBL) is a teaching and learning style that addresses many of the deficient elements in these kinds of scenarios. In the PBL approach, students are presented with an ill-structured problem and instructed to work in small groups to arrive at some resolution to the problem. The teacher is no longer the focus of all that happens, although the teacher plays a crucial role in selecting the problem and facilitating the student groups. Rather, students start to develop self-directed learning skills as they determine the kind of content learning required to move forward, the resources to use, and how new information is synthesized toward resolution. Students must work interdependently, determine multiple possible solutions, and test their ideas for viability. As a result, the students are an active part of their own learning, create their own direction as driven by the problem scenario, and continuously respond and react to each other as well as to the teacher and to the new content information they encounter.

PBL enlarges the scope of learning opportunities for students at all levels of education. Though PBL originated in medical schools, there are various organized movements nationwide to integrate the methodology in K-12 classrooms. PBL is becoming well established as a valuable addition to traditional teaching methods and has moved beyond the "flavor-of-the-month" trend so often seen in educational reform attempts.

There are currently very active initiatives to implement PBL in K-12 classrooms. These initiatives are largely grounded in the notion that PBL greatly enhances comprehension, social skill development, content retention, student motivation, and abilities to self-direct, and it engenders positive attitudes toward lifelong learning. The success of these experiences, from the kindergarten level through the high school grades, is promising and exciting.

One example of a plan to use PBL in education reform is in the mission of the Center of Excellence for Research, Teaching, and Learning (CERTL) at Wake Forest University School of Medicine. Its mission includes providing intensive and continuous professional development for K-12 educators in PBL and sponsoring enrichment programs anchored in PBL activities for

K-12 students. The CERTL has also sponsored the development of PBL instructional materials by teachers for teachers and manages the dissemination of those materials for classroom use. Examples of these classroom materials are found throughout this book.

Another example of educators' extensive interest in PBL is the participation of nearly 400 college faculty at an international PBL 2002 conference hosted by the University of Delaware. Twenty-four countries and 43 states were represented. Without question, at least several thousand schools and colleges are interested in including PBL in their teaching repertoire. In the past 10 years, several hundred U.S. schools have included PBL in their repertoire, and several books on PBL in K-12 education and teacher training have been published (see References).

This book is designed to familiarize educators with the philosophy of PBL, to show its intended benefits, and to present many classroom examples. The focus is on the use of PBL in middle and high school classrooms. Examples of PBL problem scenarios and the ways they are used by experienced PBL teachers are provided. The experiences of these PBL teachers will demonstrate the variety of possibilities for integrating PBL into current teaching strategies.

Acknowledgments

A significant number of individuals have contributed to making this book a possibility. I thank each of them for sharing so unselfishly of their time, energy, and experiences. I also thank them for their commitment to improving the quality of education for all learners and the inspiration they provide to me on a daily basis.

I express the deepest appreciation to the many, many teachers who committed hours of their time and creative energy to authoring PBL problems over the last 7 years. It never ceases to amaze me that these folks can spend a full day teaching and nurturing children and then work another 4 hours, with seemingly endless energy, to create instructional materials in hopes of making lessons better and more meaningful for students.

My thanks also go to Townley Sledge and Margaret Connor for all their assistance in locating and delivering materials at every request I made. Their commitment as pioneers in uncharted PBL territory should also be acknowledged. Nearly 10 years ago, they were members of the first teacher team to author PBL cases for this project, and they have remained steadfast in their efforts ever since.

I am constantly grateful to Dr. Patrick Ober for his leadership and support of my endeavors. It is his encouraging guidance, often delivered in the true style and guile of Mark Twain, that reminds me, "Life does not consist mainly, or even largely, of facts and happenings. It consists mainly of the storm of thought that is forever flowing through one's head." And although Mark Twain said it, Pat Ober inspires it.

Last but not least, I wish to thank Faye Zucker, editor at Corwin Press, for her patient guidance and always helpful feedback throughout the process of writing this book.

In addition, Corwin Press thanks the following reviewers for their contributions to this volume:

Robert Delisle, EdD
Lehman College, City University of New York, Bronx, NY

Sara Sage, PhD
Indiana University, South Bend, IN

About the Author

Ann Lambros, PhD, is Director of the Center for Excellence in Research, Teaching, and Learning at the Wake Forest University School of Medicine, where she is also a faculty member. Her extensive experience with problem-based learning (PBL) began in 1987 when the medical school adopted a PBL curriculum for medical students. Since then, she has conducted more than 150 professional development seminars in PBL for faculty in professional schools, 4-year universities, community colleges, and K-12 institutions. She now spends much of her time as a consultant in developing PBL curricula at every level of formal education, from kindergarten through professional and graduate school.

She can be reached at the Center for Excellence in Research, Teaching, and Learning (CERTL Office) at the Wake Forest University School of Medicine, Medical Center Boulevard, Winston Salem, NC 27157, USA; telephone: 336-713-7723; email: alambros@wfubmc.edu

1

Problem-Based Learning

What and Why

*You can memorize your way through a labyrinth
if it is simple enough and you have the time and
urge to escape.*

*But the learning is of no use for the next time
when the exit will be differently placed.*

—Unknown

Knowing What

Getting started in any conversation about problem-based learning (PBL) requires knowing exactly what is being called PBL. There are many interpretations of the methodology and just as many descriptions of what it is. For the purposes here, the following working definition is provided to support a framework for better understanding what PBL is and why it enhances traditional teaching approaches.

PBL is a teaching method based on the principle of using problems as the starting point for the acquisition of new knowledge.

1

Pivotal to its effectiveness is the use of problems that create learning through new experience, new content acquisition, and the reinforcement of existing knowledge. Situations that are in the students' real world or that they can recognize as part of their relevant future are presented as problems and stimulate the need to seek out new information and synthesize it in the context of the problem scenario. To underscore the real-world nature of the problem, students are given a specific role in the problem scenario that enhances their ownership with working toward its resolution.

Here is a simple and familiar real-world illustration of PBL. Consider the last time you required driving directions to some-where you had never been. You begin the process with what you already know, or your existing knowledge: where you will start driving and where you intend to arrive. You then identify what you need to know to effectively and efficiently reach your destination: names of streets and highways, distinguishing land-marks to look for, and perhaps the mileage you should antici-pate. You then integrate this information with your existing knowledge; for example, the amount of time it typically takes you to travel the number of miles and the type of road condi-tions you can expect. Often, after creating the experience of using the new information to travel a new route and successful arrival at the appointed destination, you can later retrieve this new information and apply it to similar situations. It is also likely that you will retain much of the new information and be able to successfully travel the same route again when the need arises.

The real-world frame of reference for you in the example above is that it is likely you have had to acquire and follow driving directions unfamiliar to you before. Each learner has his or her own real-world frame of reference that should be attended to when PBL problem scenarios are developed and used in the classroom. That frame of reference for a 12-year-old is obviously quite different from that of a 17-year-old, but it is just as significant for the effective use of PBL. It is helpful to understand the learner's real-world frame of reference when determining the role the student will assume within the problem scenario. For example, 12-year-olds still enjoy fantasy as part of their entertainment, and a PBL problem scenario might give them a futuristic or fantastical role. They might be assigned a role in the problem as a future space explorer or as a member of an undersea research community. Seventeen-year-olds, on the other hand, are beginning to see themselves as adults and are more attracted to realistic roles. They may be assigned the role of engineer or landscape architect. It is important to remember that for PBL problems to be most effective, students should be able to engage or identify with the role they have been assigned.

There are further characteristics that define and determine the quality of how PBL shows up in classroom instruction. It is essential that the learners determine their own learning needs, or learning issues, based on the problem they encounter. This is the student-centered element of PBL. In the earlier driving example, imagine that someone else determined the directions you needed without taking into account your own existing knowledge. The information they decided to provide you could discount your starting point, your familiarity with some of the route, or your own travel preferences. In essence, they would be telling you what they think you need to know, with little regard for what you think you need to know. To get excellent information, you must get answers to the questions that will help you. As the learner, you are the one who should frame these questions and then seek out the information. It is this part of the process that creates higher retention of new content and better recall at a later date.

Effective PBL lessons are facilitated for learners to determine what they need to know in order to proceed with resolving the problem. The new content that is intended for learners to pursue is embedded in how students will get to problem resolution. Curriculum standards and content objectives are linked to the problem-resolution component of this process. So, if the content standard in the driving example is "Students will know where Maple Avenue is located," then finding Maple Avenue will be an integral component of resolving the problem students are given, perhaps as a cab driver who must get from point A to point B in the shortest distance. This allows learners to frame the question, "Where is Maple Avenue?" so it is meaningful to them in relation to what they already know about the location of point A and point B. Now it becomes important to them to know where Maple Avenue is because they have decided they need this information to fill out their knowledge base regarding this problem.

Unfortunately, as educators we typically spend quite a lot of time telling our learners what they need to know without first determining what they already know or what they think they need to know. Rarely do we ask students to frame the questions that align with the type of information we think is important for them to have. Rather, we provide students with information we have already deemed relevant through lectures, handouts, worksheets, or assigned readings. In PBL, the process is somewhat reversed. Through the problem, students determine what is relevant, make that declaration, and then seek out the information they need. As the teacher using PBL problems, you will be able to accurately anticipate the students' learning needs based on the problem you have selected.

Teachers are often nervous about this notion of allowing students to determine what they need to know or which learning areas they will pursue. These questions are often posed by the inexperienced PBL teacher: How do you know that students will come up with appropriate learning issues, or how can a teacher be certain that the intended content areas will be included? PBL problem scenarios do not stand alone but are designed and facilitated by the teacher. Well-constructed problems coupled with effective facilitation will prompt students into the intended learning areas. In this book you will find examples of effective PBL problem scenarios and instructional units by grade level, the qualities and characteristics of effective PBL problem scenarios and their development, and strategies to ensure effective facilitation of PBL problems.

Collaboration and Differentiation

The PBL approach requires that students work in small groups to attain their learning objectives. Teachers will be further reassured about how learning issues are identified when they observe that within groups, the learning needs tend to be somewhat diversified. The learning needs of one student complement the learning needs of another as the group works together to address all the learning issues. A host of noncognitive skill development opportunities occur within the context of the small group. Students learn the skills of negotiation, mediation, and cooperation. They learn to organize themselves and their work, to self-direct in their learning, and to determine which resources are credible and reliable. Interpersonal skills in the areas of communication, mutual respect, and mutual consideration are developed in the cooperative nature of the groups. Students learn the art of contribution, they learn how to assist others in contributing, and they learn to distinguish valuable contributions and to acknowledge others for making them.

As these small groups become the focus of the learning situation in classrooms, teachers must assume a different and sometimes unfamiliar role. Rather than being the sole content authority in directing the learning process, the teacher now becomes the facilitator or coach of each small group. Suggestions for effective facilitation skills are offered throughout the book.

Collaboration within the group is an element of PBL that is necessary to accomplish problem resolution. This is a lifelong skill that makes sense to begin developing and practicing as early as kindergarten and certainly needs to be sponsored in the classroom by the middle and high school grade levels. The type of intended collaboration in the small group includes resource identification, peer support, acknowledgment and continued reinforcement of existing knowledge, and assistance and assurance in integrating and synthesizing new information. The formation of small groups, their dynamics, and how well they function are all important considerations in the PBL process. Because these elements are dependent on the learner's developmental stage, the principles to consider are presented in later chapters as they relate to grade level.

The last essential element of PBL is that in the process, students must take responsibility and be held accountable for their own learning. Once the students have identified their own learning issues, it is fundamental to the success of PBL to make them accountable for that learning in meaningful ways. Students must be able to demonstrate that within the process, they have acquired new content and that they can apply that new information toward problem resolution. Creating the situations that allow students to acquire new content and demonstrate application constitutes an entire chapter dedicated to authentic assessment strategies.

PBL Provides Relevance to Learners

There are philosophical underpinnings to the PBL process that explain why one would choose to make a shift to PBL in the classroom. In *How to Use Problem-Based Learning in the Classroom* (1997), Delisle gives a thorough and informative description of PBL. He describes its historical development and medical school origins. Consideration of learning theories and their alignment with PBL is provided. His book is rich with background that helps anchor the philosophies behind PBL. In this book, however, the focus is a more practical overview of why shifting to PBL practices in the classroom creates advantages for both the learners and the teacher.

PBL creates opportunities in the classroom that traditional approaches simply do not. Perhaps the most significant is that the relevance of the learning is highlighted for students. Because the problem scenarios have a real-world frame of reference, they are centered on an event that the students can imagine in their own life or in their future. The students then determine their own learning needs to understand or resolve the problem. Now, because the students have determined for themselves this "need to know," the learning that occurs is highly relevant. This contributes to holding the students' interest, developing a deeper understanding of the content, and increasing the retention of new information. It also contributes to eliminating the ever-present question, "Why do we need to know this?"

The emphasis in PBL is on conceptual understanding rather than the memorization of facts. The intended learning is presented through the problem scenario in a way that compels students to want to know and need to know the new information, much like the driver who needs directions. The problem then requires the students to use the new information to present resolutions to the problem. As the students work in their small groups toward solutions, they must collaborate and negotiate within the group to rule in and rule out viable solutions. They learn to be in functional relationships with each other to accomplish the group's goals. Students develop communication skills and more sophisticated interpersonal skills. They develop respect for one another's contributions and find ways to acknowledge and encourage each other.

In addition to these benefits, students report that they become excited about resolving the math or science or political problems and about discovering new information that helps in figuring out what is going on in the problem. Discovery, fun, and excitement are all elements that most learners prefer to have as part of instruction. We tend to work harder and longer on the endeavors that we enjoy. When students work longer and harder, they learn more and are more likely to be able to use the new information in similar contexts and situations at a later time. Also, teachers are assured that students have learned when they can apply new content.

Another outcome for students is the development of a process for lifelong learning. Students become aware that they are able to figure out what they need to know, find what they need to know, and use this new information to create solutions in situations that have no obvious answer. They grow more confident in their abilities in these areas and soon are engaging the process even outside the classroom.

A high school student recently shared the story of how she used the process for beginning a search for colleges that would best suit her. She first made a list of what she knew: the major curriculum she intended to study, the size of the college she thought she would enjoy most, the geography/climate that most appealed to her, and the greatest distance from home she wanted to be. She then made a list of what she needed to know: which colleges offered the major she wanted to pursue, which colleges had a strong reputation in that major, what was the tuition, where was the college located, and what were the admissions standards compared to other colleges of similar profile. She used a variety of resources, including her guidance counselor and printed information she obtained from the counselor. She used Internet searches and her local public library.

This young lady was using the process of determining what was known, what additional information was needed, and what resources were available. The significance of this example is that the student applied the process she had become familiar with in her classroom to an issue in her everyday, real-world life.

PBL Teaches Lifelong Problem-Solving Skills

This leads us to yet another significant benefit of using PBL. In this student's example, she was not focused as much on coming up with one right answer or solution to the dilemma of college choice as she was on obtaining the most useful information to expand her consideration of choices. PBL is specifically designed for students to focus on coming up with multiple solutions rather than one "correct" answer. The value of right or correct information as it contributes to problem solving is not negated. The intention here is not to detract from the use of accurate information such as $2 + 2 = 4$. But the value of knowing that $2 + 2 = 4$ is in how that information can be used toward problem resolution rather than in just knowing it to be so.

Focusing on multiple solutions rather than on correct answers allows students to be successful in ways that have not been available to them in traditional approaches. There are limited opportunities to be considered successful in most classrooms. Success tends to be defined by the highest scores, the most right answers, the neatest work, and, often, the most conventional work. While there is value in high scores, correct answers, and neatness, there is also value in creativity, discovery, contribution to a process, and contribution to the development of other people. Students not only are afforded these opportunities in the PBL process but are positively acknowledged as they engage the opportunities. We all have the tendency to return to and continue the things that make us feel successful. Students return to PBL each time feeling more confident, motivated, and excited about what they are able to accomplish.

The PBL Process in Action

When observing a PBL lesson, it is sometimes difficult for the novice to discern the underlying structure. Often what makes a newcomer to PBL slightly nervous is that there appears to be a very loose strategy at work. The reality is quite different, and knowing what to look for assists in providing assurance that there is a specific framework supporting the process. There are actually very specific components to the process that are there to ensure that the principles underlying PBL remain intact.

A typical PBL session begins in this fashion: The students, either as a large group or in small groups of four to six each, encounter the PBL problem scenario. The delivery of the scenario may vary from projecting the problem using an overhead projector, to a PowerPoint projection, to providing a hard copy of the problem scenario to each student or student group. For a middle school class, the problem might be as modest as this:

> Your class has decided to sponsor a family during the winter holiday season. You have raised $500 to spend for the family. Your teacher has talked with the school social worker, and together they have identified a family of four in need of assistance that has recently moved into the community. You want to provide for this family, getting the most for your money.

One student reads the problem aloud. This accomplishes several things. First, students need practice reading aloud. Eventually, they will find a comfort zone with reading aloud and will recognize that not all students know all words and their pronunciation. The idea is for them to help each other when there is an unknown or unfamiliar word. The other students in the group follow along as the problem is read aloud so there is confidence that all have heard and read the same problem without omitting key words or skipping sentences. PBL is a student-centered method, so it is always a student who reads the problem aloud.

Once the students have encountered the problem, they proceed to create a series of lists. One list is called Facts and should itemize all the facts they have been given in the problem. This helps them begin to identify what they know. In the above example, students would list things such as "We have a $500 budget; it is cold weather; there are four family members; we want to buy as much as possible for the family." They then make a list called Need to Know. Here they list all the information they would like to have to better understand the problem and their role in resolving the problem. In the current example, students might list things such as "Who are the family members; what are their ages, genders, clothes sizes; what are they most in need of; where can we get the most value for our money?" From this Need to Know list, students should begin to derive a Learning Issues list, comprised of the things they need to look up, research, or explore in order to move forward with problem resolution. The learning issues for the example would likely include "Understanding discounts; daily recommended nutritional requirements for food purchases; something about the children's developmental stages for purchasing educational toys." The Need to Know or Learning Issue list should be followed by a plan of action that will list the next steps to be taken in order to obtain new information. You will notice that a column for the plan of action is not included in Figure 1.1. This particular chart is designed to capture and blueprint the learning objectives that are pursued and how they relate to the possible solutions. The plan of action may reflect a plan for the entire group or may be individualized by each student. If you prefer to have students document their plan, then simply add a column to the format for Plan of Action. Following the exploration phase, the students should then list their possible solutions. This list will have ideas about how to resolve the problem and should require the development of a New Learning Issues list. This new list is used to gather additional information that will allow the students to rule in or rule out the possible solutions they created.

Here is a more detailed example of a seventh-grade science problem regarding weather and the process for working through it:

> You are a weather forecaster in Morehead, North Carolina. You are currently concerned about a tropical storm off the coast of Africa. You must track and predict where it is going and when it will strike land. Once you have collected this information, you must give warnings to ships and military aircraft that could be affected by the storm.

Figure 1.1   PBL Process

Facts	Need to Know	Learning Issues

Possible Solutions	New Learning Issues

Defendable Solution(s)

NOTE: This or a similar form is the basic document in the PBL process. It may be structured slightly differently or it may take two or three pages, but the categories are constant. See Resource B for examples of filled-in charts.

The students' Facts list may contain things such as "We are weather forecasters; we are in Morehead, North Carolina; there is a tropical storm, and the storm is near Africa." The Need to Know list may contain things such as "Where is Morehead, North Carolina? Where is the storm on Africa's coast? How fast is the storm moving?" There are additional facts that may be supplied to the students by providing them with maps and other information. The Learning Issues list may contain things such as "What makes a storm tropical? How are storms classified? What affects storms' movements?" From these learning issues the students might gather information about barometric pressures, ocean currents, and wind scale. They will further explore geographic issues around the landfall of the storm and where the potentially affected military bases are located. They will use mathematical equations to determine storm speed as they predict its movements. After gathering this kind of new information, students will make their list of Possible Solutions. In this case, that list might contain two or three hypotheses about where the storm will land. Then, in the context of the problem scenario, students should be provided with enough additional information about the storm's movements to eventually choose one of their hypotheses as the most viable.

Throughout this process, the teacher's role is very active as the facilitator and guide. Sometimes the teacher may take the role of "expert resource" in order to provide some of the needed information. For the most part, however, the teacher is monitoring the process and progress of the students, helping them to explore the intended learning objectives, and reassuring them or redirecting them as needed. It is important to understand that the teacher is anything but absent from the dynamics and effectiveness of this learning approach. The teacher is pivotal to the opportunities available to the students in the PBL methodology.

In a Nutshell

The intent in this book is to provide teachers with an understanding of the PBL process and with sample instructional materials to support classroom implementation. Chapters 2 and 3 address these issues by grade level, giving special attention to the developmental characteristics of middle and high school students. The additional elements that contribute to the success of PBL instruction, such as group size, group work, supporting content learning, timing, pacing, and the teacher's role, are discussed by grade level as well.

Chapter 4 describes the process for developing instructional materials that align with PBL and for creating PBL problem scenarios. The principles of problem development, format and delivery of the problem, and flow and management of the problem are presented. Issues of classroom resources, the use of Internet technology, and external resources are considered. Multiple examples are used to demonstrate the described principles and to guide teachers in their own materials development.

Chapter 5 provides an overview of the appropriate and effective use of authentic assessment techniques and PBL. Sample evaluation tools and strategies are provided as well as assessment templates specific to evaluating the students' process skills and group function levels. Guidance for evaluating students as individuals and for evaluating a student's group performance is discussed. Also included in this chapter is information about assessing the effectiveness of PBL as an instructional approach. Many teachers are concerned about being able to determine if the methodology is working in their classroom. How does a teacher know if a student is learning more, retaining more, able to apply more, or be a better collaborator or negotiator as a result of engaging the PBL methodology? This chapter also underscores the very strong linkage between local and state standards and PBL. PBL is a powerful method that can work with almost any curriculum.

The concluding chapters describe the use of PBL beyond the high school classroom setting. There is information presented that has been gathered from postsecondary educational institutions and from potential employers that supports the use of PBL to prepare students for what awaits them following high school graduation.

2

PBL in the Middle School Classroom

The objective of education is to prepare the young to educate themselves throughout their lives.

—Robert Maynard Hutchins

Getting Started

Two keys to the effective use of PBL are problem selection and facilitation. The successful execution of either or both of these keys lies in knowing the distinctive characteristics of your learners. Problems should be selected that appeal to the developmental level of your students and then facilitated in ways that produce the most response from students.

Choosing effective PBL problems for middle school students should acknowledge that the students enjoy being challenged. As this age group starts to exercise more and more independence from adults, they appreciate the opportunity to work things out for themselves. These students are developmentally ready not just to access new information but also to determine its relevance and to apply it. Selected PBL problems should allow ample opportunity for students to demonstrate their growing and more mature abilities.

Middle school students typically experience a new level of stress that accompanies this developmental stage. Evidence indicates that peer support, active decision making, and planning help reduce the stress levels these students often feel. The dynamics and activities of PBL are very effective in reducing stress among these students. These adolescent students can tackle the PBL problems that are longer in duration, richer in content, and more complex for problem-solving challenges.

The role of the student in PBL problems at this level may have them assume an adult role, engage a problem in the role of middle school student, or perhaps have them work through the problem in a fabricated role. Samples of the variety of possible roles are given in this chapter.

Another feature of PBL problems for these young learners is the opportunity for the student to discover something as the problem scenario unfolds. Developmentally, these students are attracted to scenarios of mystery and intrigue. Presenting new information in subsequent scenarios keeps students engaged in the problem over a longer period of time.

Delivering Problems to Students

The options for introducing PBL problems can be varied for middle school students. Using an overhead transparency or a PowerPoint presentation or providing the students with a written copy of the problem are common strategies. Another strategy is to have students keep a notebook of PBL problems. The notebooks double as learning journals and increase students' organizational skills. A written copy of the problem is put into the notebook, and the students document the learning issues to be pursued. The notebook is also a repository for newly acquired information and for new thoughts or ideas about problem resolution. If a problem is designed to last over many class periods or even several weeks, the notebooks support the students in organizing material and monitoring their own progress as they work through the problem components. These notebooks can become part of the assessment process as well. This assessment strategy is described in fuller detail in Chapter 5.

To deliver the problem, first divide the class into small groups of four to six students. Teachers should pay attention to group composition and how that composition potentially affects group dynamics and function. Groups should be balanced for academic talent, extroversion and introversion characteristics, and the avoidance of cliques within the group. Following the problem introduction, the groups will make the Facts, Need to Know, Plan of Action, and Possible Solutions lists. The teacher moves from group to group to be certain that the students consider things that will lead them to the intended content or objectives of the problem. Students should include in their plan of action a list of potential resources for the research they are about to begin. This list will contain many possibilities, only some of which will be used. Students should start to develop the skills for discerning credible sources of information, for the effective and efficient access of those sources, and for how to synthesize information from various sources.

Students will need to revisit their lists often and to revise them as needed. As they bring new information to the problem, the lists of Facts, Need to Know, Plan of Action, and perhaps the Possible Solutions list will change to reflect what students know and how they understand additional content. Students should be prompted to revisit their lists until they do so independently of the prompt. This is an essential step in the critical reasoning process, and it is important for the teacher to ensure that it becomes integrated into the process.

Monitoring and prompting several small groups of students simultaneously feels slightly unnatural to many teachers. This kind of group work can appear quite chaotic, has the tendency to get loud, and students do not always appear to be "on task." The students will get better at the process and more organized in their approach to problems the more often they do it. Of course, problems will vanish rather quickly if students have had PBL experience in earlier grades. However, if that is not the case, teachers will need patience as they gain experience introducing PBL, and they will be rewarded by how much students are learning, producing, and demonstrating as a result of their group work. Teachers will also develop a rhythm for moving among the groups to monitor progress and guide the students as needed. Resource C contains suggested Facilitator Do and Facilitator Don't behaviors that might be a useful reference while getting started.

Remind yourself that the PBL process has a specific structure, and be aware of where groups are in that framework. Guide them to the next step as you determine when they are ready to move forward. When they turn to you for specific information or guidance, ask them questions such as "Should that question be on your Learning Issues list?" "Have you considered any ideas that might explain this problem?" or "Have you begun to think of possible solutions?" "What do you think would be a good next step to find out?" Students may need to be reminded that they need items on their Possible Solutions list to focus them during the information gathering that will rule in or rule out their hypotheses about problem resolution.

Problem Examples

Here are four examples of PBL problems for middle school students. Additional PBL problems appropriate for these grade levels may be found in Resource A.

The first example, *Teresa and Carl,* appeals to these students because it presents a mystery to be solved, is a story line about a couple (an interest they are developing), and puts them in an adult career role that is unfamiliar but intriguing. It was designed for use in a seventh-grade classroom, but the objectives can be easily modified for use with other grade levels.

The intended objectives of this problem include understanding genetic diseases and symptoms, sex-linked diseases, heterozygous versus homozygous traits, DNA, chromosomes, mitosis, meiosis, and the role of a genetics counselor.

The problem may be read within the large group or distributed to students already in their small groups. Students should first identify the facts as given to them. This list will include the family members who are known to have the disease, the symptoms related to the disease that were overheard, and the fact that students are in the role of genetics counselor. Students will

---

Box 2.1 Teresa and Carl

You are a genetics counselor. You have an appointment with new clients today, Teresa and Carl. They are engaged to be married and have come to you with this concern:

At their engagement party, Teresa and Carl both overheard different family members talking about relatives with "the disease." They never overheard the name of the disease but did hear that Teresa's father and maternal aunt both have the illness. Carl overheard that his uncle and maternal grandmother have it as well. The symptoms that they heard described include intense pain in different parts of the body, fatigue, and shortness of breath.

Because it seemed like such a sensitive subject to those discussing it, Teresa and Carl are reluctant to ask their family members any additional questions. Instead, they have come to you for information about whether they may have already inherited the disease. They also want to know if they could pass it along to their own children, even if they show no signs of the illness.

What additional information would you like to have?
How will this information help you?
What will you do next?

---

then develop their list of Learning Issues or Need to Know items. The list of Learning Issues usually contains questions about inherited diseases, detecting existing disease, predicting the effect of parental diseases on children, and what symptoms reveal about certain diseases. Students should also question the role of the genetics counselor, but that usually comes up later in the problem. Typically, students first want to solve this mystery, and then determine how best to advise Teresa and Carl and exactly what their role is in doing so.

Students will often indicate the need to know something about the couple's background such as age and ethnicity. Some teachers choose to simply provide this information to the students when asked. Other teachers have provided the students with a set of photographs of what the couple might look like. Photographs are usually taken from a magazine and have included African American couples or couples with characteristics that might, for instance, suggest Jewish heritage or couples with Norse features. The students do not know with certainty at this stage which couple is actually Teresa and Carl. Different student groups may be given different photographs to consider, or each group may receive all three sets of photographs. Groups will then explore diseases linked to the physical characteristics of the couple and begin to rule out certain couples as possibilities.

The groups usually discover early in their research that they will need blood samples from Teresa and Carl. The results of the blood tests are included in this problem. The teacher distributes this information to each group as they identify the need to know it. Once this information is given to the students, they will need to revise their lists. They will have a lot of new learning issues regarding the information in that report. Students will need to determine, again, how they will find the kind of information that they need to move forward with resolving the problem.

Through their research efforts, the students will eventually rule out all potential diseases except sickle-cell anemia. They must then determine how to counsel Teresa and Carl regarding their own health and their question about having children.

This problem is designed to last approximately 1 week using a 50-minute class period each day. The problem often concludes with students from each group role-playing the counsel they give to Teresa and Carl. Teachers encourage the groups to include poster graphics to help the couple understand their situation. Two students in the group take on the role of the couple; one becomes the genetics counselor, and the other group members are brought in as expert consultants to assist in the explanation of the scientific data to the couple. The students not only enjoy this component, but the learning continues as the different groups often explain additional factors that may not have been pursued across the groups.

As in the preceding problem, the complexity of problems that will engage middle school students usually requires some preparation, such as collecting the photographs mentioned. Teachers should also anticipate the resources the students may need, set up related activities and labs, and have a distinct sense of the directions in which they will guide the problem and the students.

Some of the more experienced PBL teachers turn students' questions about one thing or another into a PBL problem. The teacher then lets that problem drive the learning to answer the presented questions. These teachers, however, are generally the exception, creating PBL problems on the spot. Most teachers prefer to look over prepared problems or to prepare problems well in advance of implementing them in the classroom.

PBL Problem Sources

There are two primary sources for prepared problems. One of those is from the problems developed by other PBL teachers. Many schools keep a file of these. Another source is to prepare one's own problems. Chapter 4 addresses the specifics of authoring your own problems. In the meantime, here are three more examples of PBL problem scenarios that have been used successfully in middle school classrooms. They have been chosen in addition to the previous example to further illustrate the range of roles appropriate and attractive to middle school students.

Remember, for each example in the book, teachers will use the form in Figure 1.1, emphasizing those areas teachers feel are most important for a particular lesson.

This next PBL problem, *Player's Choice,* appeals to middle school students largely because it puts them in control of a design that is almost always relegated to an adult authority figure. In this case, that adult is typically a coach. These students may have had some experience with a coach themselves, have watched sports and criticized coaches' decisions, or heard their parents do the same. In this problem they get the opportunity to advise the coach.

The objectives for this problem include understanding averaging or finding the mean, ratio/percent, rounding, graphing, statistical analysis, and applying statistics to a game strategy.

The students are given statistical information about each of the players. The teachers who developed this problem used the existing statistics of the top 15 NBA players, omitting player

Box 2.2 Player's Choice

You are the statistician for a new NBA team. Your owner has asked you to analyze the data of the team's 15 players. You are then to advise the owner of what you think would be the five best starting lineup players for the team this season. The team owner has asked that you provide graphic presentations along with your recommendations.

What would it be helpful to know about each player?
How will this information help you?
What will you do next?

names. This information can be obtained from a number of sports-oriented Web sites. The one used for this problem contains the statistical information for the top 50 NBA players. The Web site address is www.nba.com and features a link to the players' statistics. For this problem, the statistics are provided on 15 different attributes, such as number of games played, field goals attempted and made, three-point shots attempted and made, free throws attempted and made, assists, offensive rebounds, and defensive rebounds. As the students are analyzing this information, they receive an update from the owner (see Box 2.3).

Another update may be provided to students as they continue to work on their analysis.

Box 2.3 Player's Choice, Scenario 2

Player 6 has just been placed on suspension for failing a drug test. The owner needs an update on Player 6's average number of points. He also asks for a visual presentation from the coach by next week to present to the stockholders for justification on keeping Player 6 on the team. The coach needs your help to prepare this information.

Box 2.4   Player's Choice, Scenario 3

Player 11 has just been traded. You are to choose a new player to recommend to the owner as a replacement. You are limited to a pool of free agents who are currently available midseason.

Students are then given the information available on the pool of free agents. This information contains the same statistical data they have for the original 15 players.

Each group will recommend their dream team in a presentation at the conclusion of the problem. They must defend the choices they have made and use their statistical analysis to support their selections. They must also apply this information to an appropriate game strategy given the lineup they are recommending.

At the conclusion of all the presentations, the teacher reveals the identities of the professional players whose statistics were used. Students are often amazed at who they eliminated from their dream team and who they retained. There is a powerful lesson in this component as students realize the value and the limitations of using statistical analysis alone. Teachers often use this opportunity to relate the interpretation of statistics to other areas of the students' lives. Nearly every student can think of a sentence they have overheard indicating that "Statistics show . . ." Students gain insight about understanding, trusting, and questioning the use of statistical information in decision making. They learn that there may be such other factors as leadership, cooperation, or inspiration that play a role in determining the starting team.

Resource B provides samples of the PBL process charts as they might relate to this problem. Several charts are provided to illustrate the use of this problem over 3 days of instruction.

The next example appeals to middle school students because it puts the problem in their existing real world. In other words, the students are themselves in this problem scenario. Its additional appeal is that it gives the students some independence and a voice in decision making in their own home. This problem is called *More Room*.

Box 2.5 More Room

Your parents have decided to build a new house and want everyone in the family to have a part in the process. Your role is to create and plan your own bedroom, which may be as much as 20% larger than your current room.

The objectives in this problem include measurements, area, scale, percentage of increase, and averaging. Students receive additional scenario information regarding the amount of money they can spend in selecting floor coverings and any other design considerations above normal construction costs. Their product is a scale drawing of both their current room and their newly designed room. The problem is distributed to groups of students, but each student will produce scale drawings specific to his or her own current room and design for a new room. The group function is to explore and help each other understand the concepts of the intended objectives.

In this last example, students are given a fabricated role. This particular problem uses a futuristic role that appeals to the sense of fantasy most of these students still possess. Middle school students have developed beyond juvenile cartoon fantasies but still have a very active imagination that plays into these "pretend" roles. This problem is titled *Moon Messages*.

Box 2.6 Moon Messages

You are an inhabitant of the moon colony Luna. You wish to send a message by spotlight to your friend on Earth. You must determine at which phase of the moon your message will be best viewed.

The objectives in this problem include understanding the relation of the lunar orbit to phases of the moon, how light travels, the rotation of the Earth on its axis, the rotation of the moon on its axis, and the revolution of the moon around the

Earth. There are activities included in this case that help students understand moon phases and cycles. The final product for students is a model of the phases of the moon, a schedule of the phases of the moon for the next month, and a letter written to the friend alerting them when to watch for the message.

These problem examples demonstrate the interdisciplinary nature of PBL and how curricular objectives across subject areas can be included in a single PBL problem scenario. More discussion of the use of PBL to align with national, state, and local curriculum standards is included in Chapter 4.

Further Considerations for Middle School Classrooms

- A PBL problem may be used to introduce a unit of study, wrap up a unit, or be dispersed throughout instruction. The length of time a teacher chooses to use a PBL problem can be based on the problem itself, the maturity of the students, and on how the teacher chooses to guide the problem. Two of the four PBL problems in this chapter demonstrate the possible use of additional information to manipulate the length and complexity of a problem.

- As a teacher develops the ability to predict how students will respond to different types of PBL problems, problem selection becomes easier. Remember that broad problems with many potential learning issues are initially more difficult to facilitate but are typically more challenging to the students. Focused problems generally provide the students a clearer direction for their learning and achieve very specific learning objectives.

- Students in the middle level grades are attracted to PBL problems that give them the opportunity to demonstrate how they would handle a problem, independent of adult decision makers. Using multiple scenarios or new information within a PBL problem helps these students gain the insight that problems are rarely as straightforward as they may seem on the surface. Teachers should encourage students to reflect on and express how the new information affected their way of thinking about a problem.

- Middle school students are capable of doing in-depth, independent research. It is important that they experience a variety of information sources that they identify. Among these sources, they should begin to discern how to determine credibility. This is especially true in the case of Internet sites. It becomes increasingly important that students be able to distinguish a reliable Web-based resource from those that might provide questionable information.

- These students are becoming more interested in what their future as adults might hold. They may be considering college, careers, and romantic relationships in ways that are new to them. They can be especially engaged in PBL problems that require them to explore these different dimensions of maturing. For example, in the case of *Teresa and Carl*, it is not such a stretch for the students to consider themselves part of an engaged couple contemplating having children one day.

- Effective PBL problems for this age group often incorporate the opportunity for students to teach other students. They may develop lessons that align with the problem and give the information to the other small groups within their own class. Another successful plan for this strategy is to create a problem for these students to design and deliver areas of instruction to younger students in other classrooms. These older students especially enjoy this activity, and the younger children in other classrooms like this interaction.

- Middle school students are developing a higher awareness of their own independence and a desire to be more responsible. This is a good time to use PBL problems that include service-learning projects in the school and community, ethical issues, and current events that have a controversial dimension.

- Most of the labs and activities teachers currently use are appropriate for use with PBL problems. The critical consideration is how to integrate the project or activity in a PBL scenario so it correlates with the intended objectives of the problem and directly aligns with the problem scenario. Laboratory exercises and other activities should help the students achieve better understanding in their learning or discover something new that appears on the Need to Know list.

- Teachers should occasionally feel free to retreat from the PBL process if they feel it is not working. It is important to determine why the process did not work well and then try it again at a later time. Consider the time of day, the students' energy level, the complexity of the PBL problem, how well the students could relate to the problem, and/or if additional resources were needed to make the problem effective.

- A concern that teachers often raise has to do with behavior issues when students are working in small groups or without very specific direction. There is sometimes the assumption that students will take advantage of the small group activity to socialize or be off task or that they will not accomplish intended objectives without the usual type of guidance and direction. Experienced PBL teachers report that these concerns tend to be unfounded. In their experience, using PBL actually eliminates some behavior problems because many behavior problems occur when students are bored, distracted, or disinterested. Students in the middle school age groups are also becoming more concerned with peer pressure and will want to perform in their groups in ways that are appreciated. Well-designed problems and appropriate facilitation will keep students engaged in the problem and focused on its outcome. Remember that problem design and facilitation are the keys here. Using PBL does require careful preparation and active coaching. The small groups allow for more equitable participation by students than the typical large group classroom setting. When students are active participants in the direction and outcome of their learning and are genuinely busy, they have little time or cause to be disruptive or off task.

- Teachers should bear in mind that PBL offers opportunities for cognitive, psychological, and emotional development in ways that many traditional approaches do not. However, PBL is not an answer to all educational issues. As questions arise about what to do when using PBL if certain controversial issues do present themselves, teachers are reminded to consider what they are currently doing to manage those issues. Often, the strategies that are already in place will work very well alongside PBL instruction.

3

PBL in the High School Classroom

Teachers open the door, but you must enter by yourself.

—Chinese Proverb

In the Beginning

As mentioned in Chapter 2, there are two primary elements to the effective use of PBL in the classroom: problem selection and facilitation. Effective problem selection ensures that your students are interested and engaged in the problem while pursuing the learning objectives that you have selected. Effective facilitation accomplishes the same things plus assists you in classroom management issues while using PBL. It is helpful to remind yourself of the distinctive characteristics of your learners when you select PBL problems. Problems should be selected that appeal to their interests and current social development and then facilitated in ways that produce the most response from students.

PBL problem selection for high school students is, in many ways, easier than at the elementary and middle school levels.

Remember that what makes PBL problems so engaging is that students can see how the situation or event in the problem could occur in their own real world. With high school students, they can easily imagine themselves in a variety of careers such as police officer, nurse, architect, or landscaper that would have them need to know and use specific content. In addition to appealing to their interest and desire to establish themselves in the adult world with a real job or career, these students are also drawn to opportunities to defend their positions, ideas, and understanding. High school students typically prefer to work independently of direct adult supervision and would rather "consult" with adult authorities or experts when they feel the need. PBL allows students to exercise these kinds of preferences and accomplish selected learning objectives at the same time.

High school students may also be experiencing new levels of stress and even confusion as they consider the choices that face them beyond high school. The small group activities of PBL give students chances to talk about the issues around these stresses and confusion. While most high school students are not likely to describe "stress and confusion" as primary forces in their daily lives, evidence does indicate that discovering that others are experiencing similar feelings and events helps reduce stress levels for these students. An additional benefit to using PBL is that the process gives students a mechanism and experience for problem solving in their own life situations.

Introducing PBL Problems

Similar to the strategies described for middle schools students, the formats for introducing PBL problems to high school students may vary. Teachers may opt to use an overhead transparency or PowerPoint presentation or provide the students with a written copy of the problem. Another strategy, already described in Chapter 2 and appropriate for high school students as well, is to have students keep a notebook of PBL problems. The notebooks double as learning journals and increase students' organizational skills. A written copy of the problem is put into the notebook, and the students document the learning issues to be pursued. The notebook is also a repository for newly acquired information and for new thoughts or ideas about problem resolution. If a problem is designed to last over many class periods or even several weeks, the notebooks support the students in organizing material and monitoring their own progress as they work through the problem components. These notebooks can become part of the assessment process as well. This assessment strategy is described in fuller detail in Chapter 5.

To deliver the problem, first divide the class into small groups of four to six students. Teachers should pay attention to group composition and how that composition potentially affects group dynamics and function. Groups should be balanced for academic talent, extroversion and introversion characteristics, and the avoidance of cliques within the group. Following the problem introduction, the groups will make the lists of Facts, Need to Know, Plan of Action, and Possible Solutions. The teacher moves from group to group to be certain that the students consider things that will lead them to the intended content or objectives of the problem. Students should include in their Plan of Action a list of potential resources for the research they are about to begin. This list will contain many possibilities, only some of which will be used. These students should start to develop the skills for discerning credible sources of information for the effective and efficient access of those sources and for how to synthesize information from various sources.

Students will need to revisit their lists often and to revise them as needed. As they bring new information to the problem, the lists of Facts, Need to Know, Plan of Action, and perhaps the Possible Solutions list will change to reflect what students know and how they understand additional content. Students should be prompted to revisit their lists until they do so independently of the prompt. This is an essential step in the critical reasoning process, and it is important for the teacher to ensure that it becomes integrated into the process.

Monitoring and prompting several small groups of students simultaneously feels slightly unnatural to many teachers. This kind of group work can appear quite chaotic, has the tendency to get loud, and students do not always appear to be on task. The students will get better at the process and more organized in their approach to problems the more often they do it. Of course, problems will vanish rather quickly if students have had PBL experience in earlier grades. However, if that is not the case, teachers will need patience as they gain experience introducing PBL, and they will be rewarded by how much students are learning, producing, and demonstrating as a result of their group work. Teachers will also develop a rhythm for moving among the groups to monitor progress and guide the students as needed. Resource C contains suggested Facilitator Do and Facilitator Don't behaviors that might be a useful reference while getting started.

Remind yourself that the PBL process has a specific structure and be aware of where groups are in that framework. Guide them to the next step as you determine when they are ready to move forward. When they turn to you for specific information or guidance, ask them questions such as "Should that question be on your Learning Issues list?" "Have you considered any ideas that might explain this problem?" or "Have you begun to think of possible solutions?" "What do you think would be a good next step to find out?" Students may need to be reminded that they need items on their Possible Solutions list to focus them during the information gathering that will rule in or rule out their hypotheses about problem resolution.

Problem Examples

Here are four examples of PBL problems for high school students. Additional PBL problems appropriate for these grade levels may be found in Resource A.

The first example, *Roll Out the Barrel!*, appeals to high school students because it presents a mystery to be solved. The problem puts students in the role of Environmental Protection Agency chemist. Students have the opportunities to clear up the mystery and to be the expert in the problem. It was designed for use in high school science or chemistry classrooms.

The intended objectives of this problem include understanding chemical properties, chemical mixtures, compounds, elements, separation of mixtures, density, volume of a cylinder, mass, boiling point determinations, measurements, and units.

Box 3.1 Roll Out the Barrel!

You are a chemist with the Environmental Protection Agency. When you entered your lab this morning, one of the lab assistants told you of this call that came in earlier in the day:

A young couple has purchased a farm approximately 30 miles outside of town. They wish to convert the barn to a house, which they plan to live in. Upon exploration of the barn, they discovered several barrels of some liquid substance. Concerned about dumping the contents of the barrels, they have contacted the EPA for advice and to determine if it is safe to dump the barrel contents.

You decide to visit the site and collect samples from the barrels. You find a liquid that pours freely. You collect the samples and return to the lab to begin a series of tests.

What are some possibilities that can help identify the liquid samples collected?

How will you determine if the liquid is harmful?

What additional information would you like to have?

The problem may be read within the large group or distributed to students already in their small groups. Students should first identify the facts as given to them. This list will include the facts that an unknown liquid has been found, the couple want to dump the liquid, the couple want to know about safety/contamination issues, and the liquid pours freely. Students will then develop their list of Learning Issues or Need to Know items. This list of Learning Issues usually contains questions about identifying unknown substances, toxicity determination, testing processes, and safety issues for the lab workers. Students should also question the specific role of the EPA chemist, but that may come up a little later in their explorations. Students are likely to first want to identify the unknown substance and then determine how best to advise the couple.

Some students may become more intrigued than others with what EPA chemists actually do or are responsible for in their job. It is not only okay but desirable that as students work through different PBL problems, they may choose to more deeply explore the career associated with their role in the problem. This gives students good insights into different career options and may help inform them in choices they make for preparing for a career path.

In this particular problem, students will often indicate the need to know the results of tests that were run on the liquid. The following is the second part of this PBL scenario.

Teachers may choose to supply samples of the liquids listed above and to set up labs for students to actually perform some of the tests indicated. Performing the labs themselves usually heightens the awareness of students around the issues of lab safety, handling unknown chemicals, and ensuring the safety of others.

Box 3.2   Roll Out the Barrel! Scenario 2

After performing the tests, you have narrowed the possibilities down to the following liquids. Using the resources in your lab, you have prepared these notes:

Substance	Density (g/cc)	Boiling Point (C)	Viscosity	pH
Water	1.0000	100.0	0.890	Neutral
Methanol	0.7914	64.7	0.544	Basic
Ethanol	0.7893	78.2	1.074	Basic
Acetic acid	1.0500	117.9	1.056	Acidic
Ethylene glycol	1.1080	197.4	16.100	Basic
Acetone	0.7899	56.1	0.306	Basic
Benzene	0.8765	80.1	0.604	Basic

Using this data, can you identify the liquid?
What information will you share with the couple?

Teachers may decide to have students write up lab reports or prepare a report to both the EPA file and the couple that requested the investigation. Criteria for the report might include a defense for the conclusions drawn or substantial evidence that the results are reliable.

This problem is designed to last approximately three to five class periods of 45 minutes each. The problem could conclude with each group presenting their findings and their counsel to the couple. If students have performed the labs and different groups are given different chemicals to work with, it is especially helpful for students to hear from each group.

As in the preceding problem, the complexity of problems that will engage high school students usually requires some preparation, such as collecting liquid samples and preparing for the lab experience. Teachers should also anticipate the resources the students may need, set up related activities, and have a distinct sense of the directions in which they will guide the problem and the students.

Some of the more experienced PBL teachers turn students' questions about one thing or another into a PBL problem. The teacher then lets that problem drive the learning to answer the presented questions. These teachers, however, are generally the exception, creating PBL problems on the spot. Most teachers prefer to look over prepared problems or to prepare problems well in advance of implementing them in the classroom.

PBL Problem Sources

There are two primary sources for prepared problems. One of those is from the problems developed by other PBL teachers. Many schools keep a file of these. Another source is to prepare one's own problems. Chapter 4 addresses the specifics of authoring your own problems. In the meantime, here are three more examples of PBL problem scenarios that have been used successfully in high school classrooms. They have been chosen in addition to the previous examples to further illustrate the range of roles appropriate and attractive to high school students.

Remember, for each example and others in the book, teachers will use the form in Figure 1.1, emphasizing those areas they feel are most important for a particular lesson.

This next PBL problem, *Got Milk?*, appeals to high school students largely because it challenges them to come up with something that does not currently exist and because they are familiar with what is described as the "old design" and probably see the possibility that it could be improved.

Box 3.3   Got Milk?

Students receive this letter to introduce the problem:

Dear Sir/Madam:

We are ecstatic that you have agreed to take over our Purity Dairy account. Their newest request is one that is both challenging and exciting. For over three decades the milk jugs of Purity have looked the same. You are the one who gets to make history and redesign this traditional milk jug. The goal of this project is to make the jug both more pleasing to the eye as well as more practical. Purity wants the jugs to stack better in the grocer's cooler as well as be made with the least amount of material. We are confident that you can fulfill all of Purity's and our expectations. Now let's make history!

Sincerely,

John P. McGrail
CEO of Marketing Concepts

What would it be helpful to know about the product?
How will this information help you?
What will you do next?

The objectives for this problem include understanding and applying measurement concepts and skills involving area, perimeter, and circumference; finding the surface area of rectangular solids, pyramids, cylinders, and cones; estimating the solutions and solving problems related to volumes of rectangular solids; representing situations verbally, numerically, graphically, geometrically, or symbolically; and using a variety of strategies to solve nonroutine problems.

The students make a list of the facts they have been given and then a list of the information that it would be helpful to have to move forward with the problem. In anticipation of some of the questions it is expected that students will need answered, this second letter serves as the next part of this PBL scenario.

Box 3.4   Got Milk? Scenario 2

Dear Marketing Concepts:

We are very excited that you have agreed to help us make history as we revolutionize our milk jugs. We are confident that you have your best men and women working to come up with a creative, yet practical, new shape. Our next board meeting is in just 10 days. We are hoping to be able to propose your suggestions to the board at that time. In your proposal we will need a sketch of the newly designed jug, a separate page with the specific dimensions of the jug in inches, and a page on what material you would suggest we use to make the jugs.

We appreciate your hard work and timely response in this matter.

Yours truly,

Dennis Lee Herman
CEO of Purity Dairy

Students are then instructed to prepare their proposal into a portfolio and to include an explanation of why their design should be chosen.

Notice that even though specific mathematical objectives are intended for this problem, there is opportunity for multiple objectives to be addressed. The inquiry process and problem solving are two of those, but there is also an opportunity for students to practice writing skills. The emphasis could be on letter writing to include with the proposal or on persuasive writing to convince the audience that the proposed design is desirable. There are also science-based objectives in this problem as students consider the type of material to be used in the carton construction. Since milk is refrigerated and subject to some degradation through light exposure, students will need to consider these issues in their recommendation for material and how they will defend their selection.

One of the biggest advantages that teachers describe in regard to their use of PBL is the opportunity to address multiple objectives in one problem that usually constitutes a lesson plan. In ideal situations, different subject teachers collaborate and use one problem to address objectives in two or more subject areas. In several high schools, there are teams of teachers who collaborate in this way to engage students across several class periods with one PBL problem.

This next example appeals to high school students because they are familiar with newspapers and have either experienced some difficulty with reading them or may have criticized the design or selection of what appears in the newspaper. This problem gives students a chance to demonstrate how they would change the newspaper to make it more appealing to readers. The problem is called *Read All About It*.

Box 3.5   Read All About It

You are the new editor of your local newspaper. You have assigned your staff to prepare the front page of Saturday's paper and to make it more appealing to newspaper readers. You have told them that the most important articles must still appear on the front page and that they must bring articles to you for approval. You are, of course, responsible for selecting the articles that will be published.

What type of information does each article need to contain?

How much space is available on the front page?

What other information would you like to have before you proceed?

The objectives in this problem include understanding and appropriate use of sentence structure, grammar, organizing information, application of identified criteria, collaboration, use of technology, and measurements. Students are provided with a variety of articles that they must choose from in designing the front page of the paper. The process will require eliminating some of the provided articles. Once the front page has been designed, students learn that as editor they must send a letter to each author explaining why their article was not chosen or why it has been selected. Again, multiple subject areas have objectives addressed in this single PBL scenario.

In the last example provided in this chapter, students are in a more present-day and even more real-world role. They are helping their best friend to prove they were not speeding during a recent traffic accident. This problem appeals to high school students on a number of levels. Remember that friends are really important at this stage and defending a friend is a role that students quickly engage. High school students are typically already a bit defensive about their driving habits, and here they have the opportunity to prove the authorities have made an error in judgment. The problem is called *License at Stake*.

Box 3.6 License at Stake

Your best friend, Chris, got his driver's license about 6 months ago. Last night he was involved in an accident on the interstate and hit a guard rail. The highway patrol officer who investigated the accident charged Chris with speeding.

Today when Chris tells you about the accident, he insists he wasn't speeding. There was light rain and he thinks he just hit a slick spot and veered off the road when he hit his brakes. He thinks he got the ticket because the officer saw skid marks. Now he wants you to help him prove in court that he wasn't speeding.

Make a list of what you know so far.

What additional information do you need to help Chris?

Following their initial list making, students receive this additional information about the accident and about Chris's prior driving history.

Box 3.7   License at Stake, Scenario 2

You remember that Chris has had two tickets since he started driving. One was for speeding and the other was for failing to stop at a stop sign.

You and Chris drive out to where the accident happened. You measure the skid marks. They are 18 yards in length. You decide to draw a sketch showing the relationship of the skid marks to where the car hit the guard rail.

How will you determine Chris's speed at the time of the accident?

What evidence can be presented in court?

The objectives in this problem include understanding velocity, how to determine rate of speed, coordinate measuring method, triangulation measuring method, and scale drawing. For this particular problem, students are given the drawing of the accident scene to use as a reference for accomplishing the learning objectives. Some teachers also provide a copy of the police report, which students find most interesting and often spend quite a bit of time deciphering to understand the information reported in it. This is a good resource for them to have in preparing a presentation appropriate for Chris to use in court. Each group eventually presents their findings based on their own investigation and what they think is appropriate to present in the court appearance.

As pointed out earlier, all of these problem examples demonstrate the interdisciplinary nature of PBL and how curricular objectives across subject areas can be included in a single PBL problem scenario. More discussion of the use of PBL to align with national, state, and local curriculum standards is included in Chapter 4.

Further Considerations
for High School Classrooms

- A PBL problem may be used to introduce a unit of study, wrap up a unit, transition to a new unit, or be dispersed throughout instruction. The length of time a teacher chooses to use a PBL problem can be based on the problem itself, the maturity of the students, how the teacher chooses to guide the problem, and scheduling requirements.

- As a teacher develops the ability to predict how students will respond to different types of PBL problems, problem selection becomes easier. Remember that broad problems with many potential learning issues are initially more difficult to facilitate but are typically more challenging to the students, which may make them more appropriate for high school learners. Focused problems generally provide the students with a clearer direction for their learning and achieve very specific learning objectives.

- Students in the high school grades are attracted to PBL problems that give them the opportunity to demonstrate how they would handle a problem, independent of adult decision makers. Using multiple scenarios or new information within a PBL problem helps these students gain the insight that problems are rarely as straightforward as they may seem on the surface. Teachers should encourage students to reflect on and express how the new information affected their way of thinking about a problem.

- High school students are capable of doing in-depth, independent research, and PBL problems are a good way to develop their research skills. It is important that they experience a variety of information sources that they identify. Among these sources, they should begin to discern how to determine credibility. This is especially true in the case of Internet sites. It becomes increasingly important that students be able to distinguish a reliable Web-based resource from those that might provide questionable information. Also important for high school students is to become accustomed to acknowledging and citing their research sources in the form of references, notes, or bibliographies.

- These students are becoming more interested in what their future as adults might hold. They may be considering college, careers, and romantic relationships in ways that are new to them. They can be especially engaged in PBL problems that require them to explore these different dimensions of maturing.

- Effective PBL problems for this age group often incorporate the opportunity for students to teach other students. They may develop lessons that align with the problem and give the information to the other small groups within their own class. Another successful plan for this strategy is to create a problem for these students to design and deliver areas of instruction to younger students in other classrooms and in other school settings. These older students especially enjoy this activity, and the younger children in other classrooms like this interaction.

- High school students are developing a higher awareness of their own independence and a desire to be more responsible. This is a good time to use PBL problems that include service-learning projects in the school and community, ethical issues, and current events that have a controversial dimension.

- Most of the labs and activities teachers currently use are appropriate for use with PBL problems. The critical consideration is how to integrate the project or activity in a PBL scenario so it correlates with the intended objectives of the problem and directly aligns with the problem scenario. Laboratory exercises and other activities should help the students achieve better understanding in their learning or discover something new that appears on the Need to Know list.

- Teachers should occasionally feel free to retreat from the PBL process if they feel it is not working. It is important to determine why the process did not work well and then try it again at a later time. Consider the time of day, the students' energy level, competing schedule requirements, the complexity of the PBL problem, how well the students could relate to the problem, and/or if additional resources are needed to make the problem effective.

- A concern that teachers often raise has to do with behavior issues when students are working in small groups or without very specific direction. There is sometimes the assumption that students will take advantage of the small group activity to socialize or be off task or that they will not accomplish intended objectives without the usual type of guidance and direction. Experienced PBL teachers report that these concerns tend to be unfounded. In their experience, using PBL actually eliminates some behavior problems because many behavior problems occur when students are bored, distracted, or disinterested. High school students are well attuned to peer pressure and typically want to perform in their groups in ways that are appreciated. Well-designed problems and appropriate facilitation will keep students engaged in the problem and focused on its outcome. Remember that problem design and facilitation are the keys here. Using PBL does require careful preparation and active coaching. The small groups allow for more equitable participation by students than the typical large-group classroom setting. When students are active participants in the direction and outcome of their learning and are genuinely busy, they have little time or cause to be disruptive or off task.

- Teachers should bear in mind that PBL offers opportunities for cognitive, psychological, emotional, and ethical development in ways that many traditional approaches do not. However, PBL is not an answer to all educational issues. As questions arise about what to do when using PBL if certain controversial issues do present themselves, teachers are reminded to consider what they are currently doing to manage those issues. Often, the strategies that are already in place will work very well alongside PBL instruction.

4

And the Problem Is

Smooth seas do not make skillful sailors.

—African Proverb

Developing PBL Problems for Classroom Use

A variety of PBL problem scenarios have been included in the preceding chapters. These can be used as templates for creating your own problems. You can also refer to the additional problems provided in Resource A. Remember that they are examples and that your own problems should reflect your style and creativity. However, when you begin to write PBL scenarios, adhere consistently to the qualities that define effective PBL problems. The principles for authoring PBL problems are outlined below. Use them to get started writing your own problems and then use them as a checklist when your problems are completed.

Notice that sources for PBL scenarios are all around you. A defining characteristic of PBL problem scenarios is that they show up in the students' real world, so use that real world as a problem source. Newspaper articles, school issues, and family or social issues are relevant to students and are usually ripe with concepts that match most courses of study and local, state, or national objectives.

Aligning Developed Problems With Standards

Most states have now adopted accountability measures to ensure that state and national standards and objectives are being met. As a result, teachers must be able to demonstrate that lesson plans and classroom activities are intentionally aligned with those standards of learning. Nearly all prepared and published PBL problems, such as the examples provided throughout this book, have been aligned with these standards. Problems that you develop on your own should also be aligned with either your local, state, or national standards.

There are several strategies for accomplishing alignment with the mandated standards. Some teachers begin with local standards to identify the objectives for a PBL problem scenario. An example of this strategy is in the problem *Read All About It* found in Chapter 3 for high school students. The state (in this case, North Carolina) defines the English Language Arts curriculum and includes specific goals and objectives. One of the goals is that the learner will inform an audience by using a variety of media to research and present insights into language and culture. Within that broad goal, the specific objectives are to (a) locate facts and details for purposeful elaboration; (b) organize information to create a structure for purpose, audience, and context; (c) exclude extraneous information; and (d) provide accurate documentation. Each of these objectives is effectively included in *Read All About It*. Additional objectives that are intended in this problem include appropriate use of grammar and sentence structure plus providing a defense for the information chosen to be included on the newspaper's front page. Remember that most PBL problems will give you the opportunity to cover many of your objectives in one subject area or multiple objectives across subject areas.

Another example of using local standards is in *Got Milk?* (also found in Chapter 3) for a high school mathematics curriculum. This problem aligns with state competencies for geometry. The major concept included in this problem is the understanding of areas of geometric shapes and determining the volume those shapes hold. The specific North Carolina state objectives found in this problem are (a) the use of operations with real numbers to solve problems in a geometric context; (b) selection of appropriate operations and application of those operations to solve problems using real numbers; (c) use of the properties of geometric figures to solve problems and write proofs; and (d) use of inductive reasoning and the tools of construction to reach conclusions. Again, each of these objectives is embedded in the problem as the students design the milk carton specific to the criteria they are given by their client. Multiple solutions are possible, but the viable solutions require the students to explore and understand the intended objectives. Again, this problem includes additional objectives found in most geometry curricula. Students will need to understand measurement; area of solid pyramids, rectangles, and cones; and the concepts of circumference and perimeter. The inclusion of multiple objectives within a problem also provides the opportunity to reinforce concepts that may have been included in previous lesson plans. This type of reinforcement throughout the delivery of instruction increases not only understanding but also retention and recall. Accurate retention and recall is critical to student performance when it comes time to apply this information during standardized testing.

The *Teresa and Carl* example in Chapter 2 shows how to use national objectives as a blueprint for problem development. For instance, *The National Science Education Standards* (National Research Council, 1996) has identified content standards at all grade levels. One of the content standards in the area of reproduction and heredity indicates that middle school students should "develop understanding of the concept that hereditary information is contained in genes, located in the chromosomes of each cell. Each gene carries a single unit of information. An inherited trait of an individual can be determined by one or by many genes, and a single gene can influence more than one trait. A human cell contains many thousands of different genes." With these objectives in mind, PBL teachers developed the *Teresa and Carl* example for middle school students. *Teresa and Carl* prompts the students to consider that genes may carry hereditary diseases and what they need to do to determine if specific traits are present within genes. Within these broad objectives are very specific content areas for the students to pursue in order to solve this problem. They must develop an understanding of genetic diseases and symptoms, sex-linked diseases, DNA, chromosomes, mitosis, and meiosis.

Getting Started

Doing something as unfamiliar as writing your own PBL problems will feel awkward and uncertain at first. The best advice is to quickly write something down. Anything you put to paper, you can go back and change later. The danger in thinking about what you want to do for too long is that you never actually get started. Try following these steps and keep in mind that you can revise what you write as often as you like.

Step One

You should first thoughtfully select the objectives that you want your problem to accomplish. These objectives will eventually translate into learning issues and will represent the new content that students will acquire as they work through the problem. Ask yourself, What do I want my students to know when the problem is completed that they do not know now? Identify and make a list of the objectives that you would like students to understand before you write the problem scenario. Consider where this information shows up in the real world the way each of the provided examples has illustrated.

Step Two

Next, create a story line that will appeal to your learners and quickly interest them in pursuing the learning objectives you have outlined. Identify the students' role early in the problem. This gives them the reason to want to know the needed information. Notice that in most of the provided examples, each problem begins with the words "You are . . ." Remember to put the students in roles that are relevant to their world, the interests they have, and their capacity for understanding the role. In *Teresa and Carl*, students were given the role of genetics counselor. This provided them with a good reason to explore reproduction and the questions raised by the couple concerning how advisable it was for them to have children of their own. Middle school students are certainly curious about reproduction issues, and this role in the problem legitimizes all the questions they might raise.

In *More Room* in Chapter 2, students were given a real-life problem of designing a larger room for themselves. This prompted students to do a lot with math concepts, and, again, they could easily consider or fantasize that the problem was real and they were actually designing themselves a larger room full of their own influence.

The example of *Moon Messages* in Chapter 2 puts the students in the role of wanting to communicate with a friend. Since middle school students have just entered a developmental phase of valuing their friends more than ever, they can easily become invested in this role as well.

The role students are given in the PBL problem will often drive the story line. Emphasize what appeals to students, not what you think would be "good" for them to do. They will do the learning that is good for them without you pointing it out, and they will be interested in doing it for their own reasons.

Step Three

As you create the story line and develop the PBL scenarios, be careful not to overwhelm the students with too much information. Inexperienced scenario writers tend to fear that students will not pursue the intended content areas unless they are directed to do so by the problem scenario. The common mistake is to overload the problem with too many facts and too much detail. It is more important to provide the students with a rich story line that will prompt their curiosity about or investment in the intended content objectives. Look to the examples in Chapter 2, Chapter 3, and Resource A to get a feel for how to avoid this common error. *Teresa and Carl* and *Player's Choice* are good examples of rich story lines. They contain a lot of information for students to use in problem solving, but they do not contain a lot of directive information that suggests what students should be doing. *More Room* and *Moon Messages,* on the other hand, are more straightforward in problem presentation, with less information provided in the story line itself. In Chapter 3, *Got Milk?* is an example of a rich story line where students must explore many areas and concepts, yet they are not overwhelmed with too much information. Also in Chapter 3, *License at Stake* is an example of a more straightforward problem that focuses on fewer objectives but captures the students' interest.

There is value in both formats. Part of problem development and selection will be dictated by what you want to accomplish with the problem and how much time you want to spend on one problem. Rich story lines usually have students make more decisions about how and where to find new information. These types of problems often extend over several class periods and need to be rich in order to hold the students' interest for several days. Briefer scenarios usually require less research and are accomplished in one or two class periods.

Step Four

The last step in problem development is to read it aloud or preview it with at least one other person before introducing it to your class. This will help you predict how someone other than yourself will interpret the problem. Ask your previewers to tell you what they think students will say they need to know and what they think the intended objectives are. Sometimes teachers know what they intend for a problem to do but they may not have translated that effectively into the problem. This quick preview often reveals if the problem needs to be revised or tweaked before introducing it to students. Ask your pre-viewers to role-play the student the problem is intended to reach. You can tell the previewers, "You are an eleventh-grade student in my chemistry class." Then give them the problem just as you will give it to students in your class. Avoid the temp-tation to first explain to them what the problem is about and what you want it to do. This will prejudice what they do with the problem, does not allow them to interpret the problem for themselves, and gives you limited insight about how effective the problem will be in accomplishing your intended objectives. Rather, do the real role-playing situation with them. Have them read the problem aloud, tell you what they know (facts) and what they need to know (learning issues). You can then determine if the problem goes in the direction you want and if you have accurately anticipated the learning areas and objectives that students will choose.

Using Resources With PBL Problems

One consideration in problem development should be the types of resources that students will need. It is important to anticipate the necessary resources and to either provide them or be certain that students will have adequate access. A lack of resources will result in student frustration with how far they can go in problem resolution. It is especially helpful to provide some resources for students when they are just beginning the PBL process. Once they have become familiar with how to research their PBL problems, they can work more independently in locating appropriate resources.

Just as PBL problems enjoy a variety of formats, so will the resources that students will use and that you may choose to make available to them. For example, in *More Room* described in Chapter 2, where students are designing a larger room for themselves, they have been given a budget to work within. One of the resources used by teachers in this problem is often a flyer from a local hardware store with prices for gallons of paint or carpeting per square foot. For this same problem, another likely resource is their math textbook, which has the formulas needed for calculating areas and drawing plans to scale. These are readily available resources that are easily provided if anticipated in advance of the problem.

However, consider the example of *Teresa and Carl*. Students may require some resources that are not as readily available. Teachers still anticipate and provide the needed resources, but it is likely that the format will be different. Students will often ask questions about the couple's past medical history, or the families' past medical history, or perhaps about the couple's current health status. This is information that is valuable to have in the students' considerations but is information that students cannot research on their own. For these types of resource needs, teachers often supply a data sheet to the students. A typical data sheet has the kind of information it is anticipated that students will raise as questions but will be unable to access. It is important to remember that this information is distributed to students only if they ask for it. Part of the PBL process is to develop good inquiry skills, and this development may be short-circuited if students discover that they can acquire new information without asking to obtain it. Be patient; students will ask for needed information when they realize they can go no further in their resolution without it. The next time around, they are likely to ask for the information sooner rather than later.

Another example of resource anticipation is in *Player's Choice* found in Chapter 2. For this problem, there is a comprehensive Web site sponsored by the National Basketball Association. Teachers may choose to bookmark the resource, print a hard copy of the relevant information, or simply suggest to the students that it is an available resource if they choose to use it.

Other resources may include a variety of magazines or newspapers provided to the students in the classroom. Access of resources may coincide with trips to the library or learning resources center, the computer lab, or even a field trip to a science museum or government agency. Human resources are also usually quite available, and once students have begun a problem, they often have a high interest in hearing from such people. For example, invite a real genetics counselor to visit your classroom while students are exploring and researching their learning issues for *Teresa and Carl*. Have the coach come by while students are working on *Player's Choice*. Or have someone come in as the CEO for the marketing group referenced in *Got Milk?* Students will appreciate how these folks are able to help them understand content and will gain insight into the roles of specific careers. They often become interested in how someone decided to go into genetics and how they prepared for that type of job. If you decide to bring in someone to role-play, such as the CEO, be sure to script them ahead of time with anticipated questions from the students.

The use of human resources in conjunction with PBL problems has been reported by teachers to be a very effective way to get information to the students and proven to be a pleasant surprise in the way these folks are received by students. Most teachers have had the experience of inviting a special guest to the classroom who they feel could really give the students good information about a topic. It is often disappointing to teachers that many students appear uninterested, and perhaps the visit was not as meaningful as the teacher anticipated. This is yet another example, however, of teachers deciding what students need to know and how they need to know it. With PBL problems, students have already engaged the topic area in a meaningful way and have questions of substance about it. This translates into very interactive sessions with outside visitors and is much more rewarding for the visitors and beneficial for the students.

Each teacher must gauge the students' access to the kinds of resources needed for problem development and be prepared to coach the students to those resources or to provide them in the classroom. This is a significant element in how effective PBL problems will be in accomplishing the intended objectives.

Cautions and Hints in PBL Problem Development

Some of the pitfalls to avoid and other hints about developing PBL problems are presented below. As with any other new activity, this one becomes smoother and less time consuming with practice. Many teachers report that once they have seen how their students respond to the use of PBL problems and how much learning takes place in the context of problems, it is well worth their time and effort to put lesson plans into a PBL format.

It is always important to know what to avoid and what may cause pitfalls in any new endeavor. Here are some of the cautions for inexperienced problem developers to consider:

- Novice writers must be careful not to create task statements disguised as PBL problems. Even veteran PBL teachers occasionally fall into this trap, often when they are in a hurry to prepare a problem. Here is an example of a task statement disguised as a PBL problem: "You are in the seventh grade in your science class. Your teacher has just explained that you will soon be studying about different weather forces. You need to understand how hurricanes develop and move." A more genuine PBL scenario, to prompt the same content objectives, would be similar to the example in Chapter 1 where students are put in the role of weather forecaster. In that example, students are concerned with the development of a tropical storm, how it might upgrade to a hurricane, and predicting where it might make landfall. In the task statement, students are simply told what they need to know, and presumably they will look those things up and be able to report on them. In the PBL scenario, students are given a responsibility with the problem for knowing the same kind of content about weather and content, but they make the decisions to know these things on their own. The PBL scenario is student directed, while the task statement is teacher directed.

- Another caution is not to give away too much information or to give too much information too soon in the process. Inexperienced PBL teachers are often tempted to give the entire story line at one time so that students will get to the intended objectives quicker. Remember that quicker is not always better, and that getting students engaged in the process is critical to its success. Give students three to four sentences at a time initially and then stop the problem to ask, "What do you know?" "What do you need to know?" "What would you like to do now?" Have students make these lists and thoughtfully consider what new information is necessary to move forward. Well-constructed PBL problems will have already anticipated their questions and be prepared to provide some of that information in the subsequent scenarios.

- A last caution is to have realistic expectations about what students will do with problems. Remember that this process is not typical of the behaviors that have been rewarded in traditional classrooms. Students will need time to become familiar with what is expected of them and what they have permission to do and explore in the PBL process. Students will get better and better at using the process, and your expectations should grow with their experience in resolving PBL problems.

Here are a few additional hints in making your PBL problems as effective as possible:

- Let students interpret the problem and their role in it for themselves. Once the problem has been introduced, students should be able to describe who they are in the problem and what is expected of them regarding problem resolution. This is much more effective than having students read the problem and then explaining to them who they are and what they should do next. In other words, let the students be in charge of the problem.

- Be prepared for the unexpected when you first begin to write and use PBL problems. Sometimes problems will take a direction that you did not anticipate. Before you redirect the students by telling them that they are on the wrong track (remember, that takes the problem away from the students), take a moment to determine if there is value in the direction students have chosen. In other words, is the path they are on going to lead them to different objectives that you will be presenting elsewhere anyway? If so, let them go in that direction. If not, simply ask them why they are headed in an appropriate direction. Sometimes they have misread the intention or misunderstood their role. A few seconds to have them reassess these two things often clears up any miscues that they may have assumed.

- The last hint, already mentioned, bears repeating here. Practice delivering new problems to someone other than your students before using it the first time in your classroom. Many teachers are tempted to skip this step and let students have the first crack at a problem. Remember, however, that you are new at this process, too. It is sometimes awkward to introduce PBL problems until you become comfortable with doing so. Saying things aloud a few times before going into the classroom helps eliminate some of this awkwardness. Decide how you will introduce the students to the PBL process and then introduce them to the problem. Give them a little heads-up on what is different in this process about what they will be doing and what you will be doing. Otherwise, it is very normal for students to sit passively and wait for you to continue rather than to get down to work themselves.

A Final Word

Once teachers become comfortable with PBL, they often opt to use PBL units to meet the curriculum goals. PBL units typically consist of three or four PBL cases that have been developed to use over a longer period of time and to include more objectives. One PBL unit for middle school students is called *Let's Go to the Fair*. It consists of three PBL problem cases: *Down-n-Down We Go, Push-n-Shove,* and *The Ramp Ride: Down-n-Over.* The emphasis of this unit is on science competency goals as defined by North Carolina for eighth graders. The goals are for the learner to understand force and motion; Newton's laws of motion gravity, time distance, mass, and force; and to incorporate math skills into problem solving. The students are put into the role of engineer and have been contracted by a theme park to develop new rides. These students enjoy theme parks, and most have visited one at some point in their lives. This problem gives them the opportunity to create the rides that they would enjoy seeing in a theme park or think that others would enjoy. This unit and the students' role in it not only maintains their interest over a 3-week period but also provides ample opportunities to include many specific objectives that fall within the described competencies.

In the first case of this unit, students must design a vertical fall ride. They receive specific criteria about the ride and must build a model or provide a demonstration of how the ride will operate. In the second case, students are asked to build a ride that demonstrates Newton's third law of motion. The park owner has special concerns over the safety features of this ride, and the students must be prepared to ensure it is safe. The last problem requires the students to restore an existing roller coaster rather than build a new one. They may change some of the design but cannot start over from scratch. They are given criteria from the existing ride to inform how they will redesign it.

These three PBL problem scenarios effectively address the specific goals of the science competencies mentioned above. In all, there are 19 specific goals embedded in this one PBL unit. Teachers often report, however, that students exceed those goals by including additional areas on the Learning Issues list. Budgeting is embedded in all the problems and is, of course, a math competency. Consideration of space available for the rides also requires students to use measuring concepts and area formulas for perimeters of different shapes; also a math competency. As the design engineer, students must develop a plan of safety for each of the rides and present it in writing to the client. Writing competencies are addressed in this manner, and oral competencies are addressed when students must present and defend their designs.

This is only one of many unit examples. When you write a PBL problem, it is good to keep in mind how it might develop into a unit by aligning one or more additional cases with it. One advantage to the use of PBL units is that it keeps students in the rhythm of inquiry-based and cooperative learning. Many of the characteristics of these strategies are not inherent to traditional classroom teaching but are desirable for student learning. Rather than have students move back and forth from these nontraditional approaches to the traditional strategies, PBL units allow students to rely more consistently on their newly developed skills. Other advantages include the fact that the use of PBL units keeps students interested in topic areas longer and allows the teacher to cover multiple objectives that are related but also distinct. Assessment of students at the end of a PBL unit also gives teachers a fuller understanding of what students have accomplished in their learning with the PBL methodology. These assessment techniques are discussed in more detail in Chapter 5.

It is most important that teachers find their own rhythm for using PBL problems or units. The teacher's comfort level will inform the students' comfort levels. One of the best ways to get comfortable with using PBL is to author your own problems and then use them with confidence.

5

Knowing You Did It

Judge a man by his questions rather than his answers.

—Voltaire

In the current climate of high stakes accountability, it is important for teachers to have confidence in the methodology used for instruction. It is just as important, however, for teachers not to succumb to the mythical notion that rote memorization of facts and formulas will increase students' performance scores. The reality is that students' scores go up when they know, understand, can retrieve, and use information in situations similar to those in which it was learned. Unfortunately, the format of most standardized tests reinforces the old memorization myth but does little to increase student learning. Consider the following analogy:

> Imagine that the basketball season consists of one game, played on the last day of the year, in which players do not know which plays they will be asked to make. Imagine also that they do not know which of their shots went into the basket until weeks later. Imagine that the scoring is understood only by the scorekeepers, not the players or the coaches. Who would improve at the game?

Of course, the obvious answer is that no one would improve. Rather than remain driven by a system that does little to improve student performance, PBL advocates that assessment strategies can increase learning, thereby improving student performance on traditional and nontraditional assessment instruments.

Making the PBL Grade With Authentic Assessments

It is important to keep in mind that assessing student learning that occurs during PBL instruction is likely to be quite different from traditional assessment strategies. Just as teachers are sometimes initially uncomfortable with PBL instruction, the same is true when it comes to assessing students in a manner consistent with PBL instruction. To assist in the distinction of traditional assessment methods from those that support PBL instruction, the term *authentic assessments* is used to describe PBL assessments.

Authentic assessments have distinguishing features that both characterize them and align them with PBL instruction. Those features include collecting evidence from multiple activities, measuring student learning by engaging them in examples of what you want students to be able to do, and continuing to promote learning throughout the assessment process.

Traditional assessments are typically an audit of performance. They often measure what students can recall on a certain day at a given time. This type of assessment rarely informs teachers of what students know and can do with what they know in the days or weeks following the test. These assessments rarely have a component that leads to improved performance. Rather, they simply measure and report ability to recall and do not include a process for addressing knowledge gaps or providing deeper feedback to the student. This is because traditional assessments also tend to focus on uncovering what students do not know. While it is important to target knowledge gaps that students may have, it is too often the case that these gaps are exposed and then left unattended. Students typically receive a graded quiz or exam with the wrong answers marked but no follow-up explanation for why answers are incorrect or further instruction to correct or deepen understanding. Additionally, traditional assessments often disrupt learning. Students will stop the learning process to memorize information or cram facts and details in order to perform well on traditional short-term recall examinations.

In contrast, the authentic assessments used to support PBL instruction often occur throughout the learning process with perhaps a culminating activity or demonstration of student achievement, such as an oral or written report, poster, or constructed model, at the end of the problem. They are designed to give the students specific feedback about their understanding and to improve the students' performance throughout the learning process. Authentic assessments reveal and emphasize the understanding that has occurred and allow opportunities to correct areas of misunderstanding or oversight.

Authentic assessments are also designed to support evaluating the critical reasoning process as well as the content acquisition of students. Effective PBL assessments evaluate each student's performance as a group member. The quality of work within each of these areas—content acquisition, reasoning and thinking process, and collaborating for effective outcomes—is considered for its value to the student's growth and the group's performance.

Working from the following examples may help in understanding effective ways to structure the assessment plan you use in conjunction with PBL.

PBL and Assessment Examples

Content assessment in PBL is designed to demonstrate the student's understanding of concepts and ability to apply that understanding. Feedback on the quality of content acquisition should be given throughout the duration of the PBL problem. The teacher provides this feedback as groups are monitored during the PBL process. The teacher may do this by asking prompting questions, commenting on what students have researched, or having the students self-assess their progress. This allows students to improve their performance during content acquisition and hopefully to deepen their understanding.

An example of a content assessment rubric is given below. This simple rubric accompanies the PBL problem *Moonball,* a middle school science problem provided in Resource A. In this problem, students are to suggest changes in the existing rules and regulations for the way basketball is played on Earth to the way it would be played on the moon. They are then asked to expand the newly formed Moon Basketball Association to an intergalactic league by making additional suggestions to adapt the rules and regulations.

Score	Criteria
5	Three changes in the rules and regulations CLEARLY explained for more than three celestial bodies. Accurately completed worksheet.
4	Three changes in the rules and regulations CLEARLY explained for at least two celestial bodies. Accurately completed worksheet.
3	Three changes in the rules and regulations CLEARLY explained for at least the moon. Accurately completed worksheet.
2	At least one change in the rules and regulations CLEARLY explained for the moon.
1	At least one change in the rules and regulations has been proposed. It does not have a clear scientific explanation.
0	No changes in the rules and regulations explained.

In this example, students must demonstrate an understanding of the concepts regarding gravitational forces. A worksheet on calculating weight changes for Earth, Pluto, Jupiter, Saturn, and the moon is provided with the problem. Students receive no credit for proposing changes in the rules and regulations that they cannot scientifically explain. Each group orally presents their proposed changes to the class or in a written format to the teacher. Students are encouraged to orally report, when time allows, even if they provide a written report. This gives students the chance to practice oral presentation and to demonstrate their ability to explain what they have learned. The teacher determines the achieved score and gives that to each group member.

Going Beyond Content Assessment

Only content acquisition has been assessed in the previous example. In PBL it is equally important to assess the process used for arriving at solutions to the problem. This component is what helps to ensure that students can transfer the process from one problem to another, enhancing their ability to apply what they learn to different situations. Because the PBL process is interdependent rather than independent, it is practical to assess the students' collaboration skills as part of their skill with the process. Forms 5.1 and 5.2 are examples of a longer rubric used to assess an individual student's group and process skills.

A similar rubric has criteria that are slightly more sophisticated in regard to the PBL process. This rubric may become more appropriate as students gain experience with the method or with older students.

The teacher rates the students on the categories given (or similar ones of his or her own choosing) as the students work through the PBL problem. Teachers are encouraged to give students feedback on the quality of their contributions in these categories as work progresses, thus giving them time to improve any areas of weakness. It is suggested that teachers make notes about individual student performances that heavily influence the overall rating. For example, if a student asks good-quality, probing questions that move the group toward better understanding, that behavior should be noted for the student. On the other hand, if a student constantly throws out nonsensical questions just to be part of the conversation and derails the process, that behavior should also be noted for the student.

These observations should be shared with the student at an appropriate time along with suggestions for improving areas of weakness. Where these observations concern areas of strength, students should be encouraged to help other students strengthen their performances in similar ways. The overall rating should be

Form 5.1 Individual Student Assessment in Group (I)

Student Name _____ Problem _____
Rate each individual's performance as: 4 = Excellent
3 = Good
2 = Fair
1 = Poor
0 = Unscorable

	Student Names				
Date:					
CRITERIA					
Participates in group work					
Contributes to project success					
Listens to others					
Asks and answers questions					
Stays on task					
Finds and contributes quality information					
Cooperates with others					
Offers positive suggestions					
Exhibits leadership					
Compliments and encourages others					
Overall Rating:					

Form 5.2   Individual Student Assessment in Group (II)

Student Name _____   Problem _____
Rate each individual's performance as: 4 = Excellent
                                            3 = Good
                                            2 = Fair
                                            1 = Poor

	Student Names			
Date:				
CRITERIA				
Generates effective learning issues				
Demonstrates hypothesis proposal and testing				
Grasps new concepts				
Applies new information				
Shows skill at teaching peers				
Demonstrates cooperation and consensus building				
Participates effectively in group process				
Identifies and shares appropriate resources				
Demonstrates growth of knowledge				
Exhibits functional, decisive, and focused qualities				
Exhibits leadership appropriately				
Encourages others with useful feedback				
Addresses own strengths and weaknesses appropriately				
Overall Rating:				

determined when the PBL problem is completed. Each student receives an individual rating on the group process performance component of assessment.

Another element of authentic assessment is in weighting the components of content acquisition, individual contribution to group process, and collaboration skills. The weight assigned to each area carries a message to the students about where to concentrate their energies and efforts. Let's say, for example, that the content assessment is to contribute to a student's overall grade for the quarter or semester in a subject area the same as a quiz score would—maybe 10%—but the individual group process score is weighted at 5%. The teacher could, of course, weight these differently in different assignments. However, with this kind of distribution, the message to students is that knowing the content is more important than contributing effectively to the group process. Students may be less concerned with sharing resources or encouraging others than they are with showing that they have learned new material. However, both are important when assessing PBL activities.

Teachers are cautioned to weight the assessments appropriately to support the PBL methodology. Another caution is to limit the assessment topic areas to three or four major categories or else the teacher will unnecessarily become an accountant.

Using Portfolios With PBL

For lengthy PBL problems, the use of a portfolio is recommended. In this design, students can demonstrate their content acquisition and their skill at critical thinking in a variety of formats. For example, a portfolio may contain a learning log where students list their need to know items or learning issues and then describe the resources used to research those. Evidence of the research, such as a report or worksheet, becomes part of the portfolio. Here is an example of a learning log for the problem *Lost Without a Cell Phone*. The problem puts students in the role of a member of the camera crew for an award-winning film company. The film company is doing a documentary on the human body, and the crew have been miniaturized and injected into a body to film. They find themselves trapped in the nucleus of a pancreas cell with no way of communicating and a failed propulsion system. They must find their way out of the cell safely. The full problem is included in Resource A.

Students receive the log as an empty grid. They complete the grid cells as they progress through the PBL problem (see Form 5.3). The column for Evidence identifies the material that they will include in their portfolio to demonstrate they have researched and understood the learning issue. Notice that at times, their evidence for one learning issue may serve as a resource for a different learning issue. This use of their own evidence reinforces students' understanding of the material and their ability to apply that understanding to problem resolutions.

The portfolio often contains a writing component that is persuasive and requires the students to defend their most viable solution. Students may support their defense by including newspaper articles, Web site references, or collected pamphlets and brochures. They may draw diagrams or pictures to demonstrate why one solution is desirable over another. The teacher determines the criteria for the writing component such as a business letter format, short report, research, or essay.

A distinct advantage of a portfolio is that it allows for assessment to occur throughout the problem in a documented form. Students may turn in the portfolio at various stages of completion and receive formative feedback. They may then have a chance to revise the earlier work in order to improve their performance, and they will have specific guidelines for the remainder of the work to be completed.

Examples of other authentic assessments that may be included in a portfolio format include observations of student performance, work samples, and projects. It is most effective to provide the students with a copy of the scoring form or checklist to be used for assessment when the assignment is made or when the PBL problem is introduced. The teacher should provide the criteria to be assessed, distinctly outlined, and, whenever possible, a model or example to be followed. Students should also understand how gradations in quality will be assessed, from not acceptable to exemplary and any categories in between.

Form 5.3   Student Learning Log

Student Name: _____ Problem: *Lost Without a Cell Phone*

Date	Learning Issue	Resource(s)	Evidence
3-13	What does the pancreas look like? What does it secrete? What does it do?	Biology books, Internet, encyclopedia	Diagram of the pancreas, list of functions
3-13	What does the nucleus look like? Where is a nuclear pore located? How does the nucleus identify waste?	Biology books, Internet, encyclopedia	Diagram of pancreatic cell showing nucleus
3-14	What is the role of the nucleolus, chromatin, chromosomes, nuclear membrane, DNA, and RNA?	Biology books, Internet, encyclopedia, *Living Cell* video	Picture and written description of each cell structure
3-14	What is the function of cell division, cytoplasm, cilia, and flagella?	Biology books, Internet	Picture and written description of each cell structure
3-14	How will we find our way out of the cell?	Diagrams and descriptions collected so far	Developed viable hypotheses

Several more examples follow for you to use as models or frameworks to design your own authentic assessment tools.

More PBL Assessment Examples

The examples that follow are primarily for assessing new content acquired by the students during PBL instruction. Keep in mind that it is strongly recommended that the teacher assess students' contributions to the group, the group process, and the quality of those contributions using one of the previous examples, in addition to assessing core knowledge. Only a thumbnail sketch of each problem is provided here, but the full problem is included in Resource A.

In a middle school math problem titled *Getting Decked,* students are put in the role of a volunteer with Habitat for Humanity. They have been given the responsibility of completing a purchase requisition for an 8' × 10' deck for the back of the home being constructed. Students learn in a later scenario that they must not exceed $500 in material purchases for the deck. Students are assessed at completion of the problem using a rubric similar to that in Form 5.4.

When using rubrics or assessment tools similar to this one, bear in mind that what you determine as an element of comprehension might also demonstrate the use of certain processes. Likewise, a performance element might demonstrate comprehension. It is not as important to distinguish one element from the other as it is to be thoughtful about what criteria are included for scoring and how each criterion is weighted in the overall assessment. Notice that in this example, the student had better-than-competent scores on all areas except the actual product, the requisition. In a traditional assessment where only the final product is considered, this student's strengths might get lost in a messy final product. However, it is important to acknowledge what the student did well to achieve that final product and to score the lack of clarity or organization on its own. Communicate this as a weakness to the student but give value to the areas where he or she demonstrated good understanding and application of important concepts.

Form 5.4   Getting Decked

Student Name: _____   Problem: *Getting Decked*
Overall Score: _____
Scale: 4 = Exemplary
          3 = Above Competent
          2 = Competent
          1 = Below Competent
          0 = Failing

Assessment Measure	Score (Weight)	Comments	Date
Performances: • Produces a purchase requisition that is accurate in materials needed and projected costs. • Produces a requisition that is easy to understand and read.	2 (20%)	An accurate requisition; hard to follow; could be better organized	
Processes: • Uses credible sources for cost figures. • Uses materials that allow for minimal waste. • Orders all materials needed to complete deck.	3 (25%)	Good job including all materials; good use of materials chosen; accurate cost figures	
Comprehension: • Stays within budget without compromising quality. • Uses appropriate math functions for determining amount of materials. • Uses appropriate math functions for sales tax calculations.	3 (30%)	These were all accurate, but you had to be reminded to include sales tax in your final cost projections	
Other: • Contributes to group function consistently. • Makes contributions of quality to group. • Meets group expectations. • Assists other group members as needed.	4 (25%)	Excellent group interactions; I really liked seeing you assist others in the group with the math equations	
Final Score	3+		

Using Self-Assessments
and Peer Assessments With PBL

Another important consideration is to have students self-assess using the same form or rubric that will be used to reach their final score. It is generally accepted that students who are better self-assessors are better performers. Sound and accurate self-assessment takes practice. By having students use the same form and criteria that you will be using, they have the chance to see how well their own assessment aligns with yours. You might discover that the student in the above example will indicate a desire for more time to have redone the requisition before turning it in to you. Or you might discover that the student does not view the requisition as messy or unclear. Either observation is a valuable one to have about your student. If students have the self-awareness that the product could have been neater or better, more than half of your work on this front is done. If they have no such awareness, you may need to show them examples of other students' work or take extra time to show the difficulty in interpreting their work in the format they used.

An additional component to authentic assessments is the use of peer assessments. Again, using the same forms that you will use, have the students assess each other's work in each of the categories or components you will be assessing. Remember, as young adults and throughout life they will be engaging in peer assessments regularly, sometimes formally and at other times informally. We all do this daily with our own colleagues, as consumers of professional services, and within our community organizations. It is important to develop accuracy in assessing others, and middle or high school is not too soon to start developing this skill. And it is important for students to understand how their work is viewed by others. It may also eventually save you some time and effort. As students become more effective at peer assessment, you can use their insights and comments to assist in your own review of work turned in by students.

This last example (Form 5.5) is from a high school anatomy case, *The Latter-Day Robin Hood.* In this problem, students are in the role of emergency room doctor when a call comes in from a young man on his cell phone. He is shouting that he and his buddy were camping and hunting in the woods when his friend accidentally got shot with an arrow. Now his friend has blood coming from nearly all of his orifices and is being brought to the hospital emergency room by his friends. You have a chance to ask where the buddy was shot but all you hear before the phone goes dead is "He was shot clean through." The students must determine what organs the arrow may have hit or penetrated to produce the described bleeding, and they must make considerations on the best emergency care to provide when the patient arrives.

For this problem, students are allowed to develop their own final product to best demonstrate the path they believe the arrow followed. They are given the following criteria in rubric form to help them determine how they will show what they have learned and how they will defend their most viable hypotheses.

In this type of format where students are given leeway in the product they choose, be careful to assess the student learning on the qualities described in the rubric rather than on the final product itself. For example, one group of students chose to use a human skeleton with different colored balloons placed as the organs and a dowel positioned as the arrow. They then described each organ, its function, why it was likely to have been punctured, and what type of patient management should be prepared in the event that the organ was indeed affected. Another group of students had a very elaborate anatomical chart that they constructed with organ overlays and printed descriptions. These are very two distinct formats, and the latter is typically more traditional than the first example. However, both groups of students demonstrated the acquisition of new anatomical content and the fact that they had fully explored all of the intended learning issues. Both groups gave very clear and precise presentations, and both had sound reasoning and references for their recommendations. The caution here is for teachers to be careful not to give more value to the more traditional product unless it better meets the criteria of the rubric. The first product was a very creative way for students to demonstrate that they met the criteria, and the value should be placed on the learning if the product format is not predetermined by the teacher.

Form 5.5   The Latter-Day Robin Hood Rubric

Component	Possible Points	Points Earned
• Logical Reasoning	4	——
Based on:	4 = cites data and literature for organ location and possible puncture 3 = fits most data with scenario and references 2 = fits half or less of the facts with the findings 1 = does not fit facts; no reasoning provided	
• Recommendations	4	——
Based on:	4 = cites data and literature for best emergent care to provide and understands why 3 = fits most data with scenario and references 2 = fits half or less of the facts with findings 1 = does not fit facts; no understanding provided	
• Presentation	4	——
Based on:	4 = clearly summarizes facts and solution in understandable form 3 = slightly unclear or confused; audience needs some clarification 2 = unclear and disorganized although some effort is evident 1 = no evidence of effort	
• Daily Grade	4	——
Based on:	4 = clearly carries thoughts and efforts in group beyond ordinary 3 = good effort; understands learning issues 2 = tries to some degree; accomplishes some work 1 = no evidence of effort	

In determining your assessment plan to support PBL instruction, it is helpful to remember that one of the PBL characteristics is the problem's relation to the real world. Consider how assessment occurs in the real world, and incorporate similar elements into your plan. This will help your students become familiar, comfortable, and skillful at being assessed in performance situations.

6

The Whole Picture

The true test of character is not how much we know how to do, but how we behave when we don't know what to do.

—John Holt

One of the most appealing aspects of PBL is its friendliness to a variety of other teaching strategies. It is important to remain mindful that PBL is not intended to be an add-on to the existing demands on instructional time. Rather, PBL is designed to complement teaching strategies already in use and to replace those strategies that may be less effective for long-term learning or less engaging to students. Additionally, the characteristics of PBL promote skill development that may be absent in more traditional approaches.

PBL provides a context for the use of the most effective teaching practices. Consider its design as a way to wrap or package other teaching concepts. Embedding a cooperative learning lesson or a service learning project in the PBL design strengthens their effectiveness for students by giving the lesson or project a real-world application. This promotes the capability of students to transfer these concepts to other situations of daily life and to other learning experiences. Examples of incorporating successful teaching practices into the PBL design follow.

PBL and Cooperative Learning

Cooperative learning, much like PBL, has enjoyed a variety of definitions and descriptions. Using the simplest of definitions from Johnson, Johnson, and Holubec (1993), cooperative learning is "the instructional use of small groups so that students work together to maximize their own and each other's learning." The principles and elements of cooperative learning capitalize on the social engagement students enjoy when they work in groups. Its design also promotes the idea of students viewing their peers as resources rather than as competitors. As described by Jacobs, Power, and Inn (2002), "The principle of positive interdependence is the most important principle in cooperative learning. Positive interdependence represents a feeling among group members that what helps one group member benefits all the members, and what hurts one member hurts them all." The challenge is to provide students with the most suitable learning environment to recognize and value these principles of cooperative learning.

The PBL design addresses this challenge by placing the small group principles of cooperative learning into a context where the value of working together is apparent and rewarded. Remember that in PBL, students are placed in a real-world role within a problem that must be resolved. Applying this strategy to the use of cooperative learning enhances the principles and power of learning in groups. Consider the following example.

Jacobs et al. (2002) provide the suggestion of using an exercise called Jigsaw to help students realize the power of learning from one another. In the example, students work in small groups called home teams. Each home team receives different pieces of information that when compiled complete a concept or learning objective. In the example provided in Jacobs et al., the student groups receive information on either the habitat of frogs, the anatomy of frogs, the feeding and reproductive habits of frogs, or threats to the survival of frogs. Students visit other groups or teams in order to obtain additional information about frogs that differs from their team's information. Team members return to the group to share what they have learned and to complete the "jigsaw" of informational pieces about frogs. The exercise emphasizes the value of learning from others, teaching others, sharing information, and researching what others know beyond your own knowledge base. These are valuable concepts to the effectiveness of cooperative learning and are also characteristics of PBL.

The use of this cooperative learning strategy in PBL actually increases cooperative learning's power and effectiveness. Here is how the same exercise might look when placed in the context of the PBL design. Small groups of students are given a problem where they are in the role of day camp counselor. (Remember, in PBL it is important the student role be one they can identify with somewhere in their own real world. It is likely that many students have been to a camp with a counselor or know of someone who has. They can use this personal knowledge or learn from their group members' experiences to understand their role in the problem.) As the day camp counselor, students have received a note from a concerned parent. The note says that their child came home from camp yesterday and described two frogs that they found on a nature hike. One frog that they found had only three legs and the other appeared to have an extra leg. The parent's concern is that there is something present in the environment causing the frogs to deform and that it could pose a threat to the children in camp. (This full problem, *Amphibian Anxiety,* is found in Resource A.)

Students will need to explore all the concepts provided in the jigsaw example—the habitat of frogs, the anatomy of frogs, the feeding and reproductive habits of frogs, and threats to the survival of frogs—in order to understand the normal development of frogs and then try to determine what might cause abnormal development. Additionally, students will need to explore environmental concerns such as contaminated water or food supplies. They will also learn how environmental toxins threaten animal habitats and if there are implications for humans in the same areas.

The jigsaw strategy works in this example by assigning different learning issues for exploration to different groups. Once students have acquired the information to address their learning issues (whether that information is provided by the teacher as in the jigsaw example or they research new content on their own), they can then share the information with other groups in order to resolve the problem they have been given.

Once each student group has acquired all the available information, they can then determine together how to respond to the parent. Each group can then present their ideas to the whole class, which extends the cooperative learning experience by providing additional insights from all class members to each other.

Using the PBL design to embed cooperative learning concepts not only enhances student engagement by giving them a role in the problem but also provides the opportunity to include integrated learning concepts by broadening the new content needed to address the problem. In this example, it did not suffice to understand only the original learning objectives about the habitat, anatomy, development, and threats to frogs. Students also had to understand what might adversely affect the habitat and development and then apply that new information in their effective communication to the parent.

When this type of instructional strategy is aligned with the types of assessments used in PBL, the power of cooperative learning is increased. Bear in mind that effective PBL assessments value how students contribute to the group, how they contribute to problem resolution, how they support each other in the process, and how much content they acquire. By placing value on these attitudes and behaviors in evaluation, students appreciate their importance throughout the instructional process.

Teachers who have used cooperative learning effectively in their classrooms are encouraged to use those lesson plans that have worked well in the context of a PBL problem. It will quickly become apparent that the complement of these two strategies boosts the benefits of each approach.

PBL and Service Learning

Service learning is not a new concept in most schools or classrooms. However, it has gained new attention as a context for enhancing character education and community volunteerism and addressing curricular objectives. Most service learning lessons involve an out-of-classroom activity that is frequently done by small groups of students. While service learning activities are highly worthwhile as they now exist, their power for addressing curriculum objectives and fostering collaboration among students can be increased using the PBL design.

In many traditional classrooms, service learning activities are assigned to students or a list is provided for students to choose an activity. Examples include adopting a park or stretch of highway for cleanup, tutoring younger children, or fund-raising for a charity or community-supported service. These examples provide ample opportunity to align with curriculum objectives by exploring the effects of pollution in our parks or along the roadways, tutoring in the same subject areas at lower grade levels, or determining cost-effective ways to raise money on a budget or without a budget. The value of these activities for classroom instruction and for contributing to the community beyond the classroom is apparent. However, the use of PBL in service learning activities raises the value on all levels enormously.

Consider this true example from a middle school classroom. Students were put in the role of volunteer coordinator and given the problem to design a nutritionally balanced menu for a Thanksgiving meal at a local homeless shelter. They were told to keep in mind that the budget was limited for the meal and it should be as cost effective as possible while at the same time adhering to nutritional guidelines. Once the meal had been determined, students were then to develop a brochure for distribution to heighten awareness that the shelter would be providing the Thanksgiving meal.

Students first had to explore the recommended nutritional requirements for adults and children. They then had to determine which foods were highest in nutrients, lowest in cost, and easy to prepare for a large group. They also considered the appeal of the foods in the context of a traditional Thanksgiving meal. Students then begin to explore food costs through local newspaper advertisements and by visiting grocery stores and discount warehouses. While the original intent of the problem was to have students address curricular objectives of food values, nutritional requirements, healthy diets, budgeting, and writing/communication objectives in the brochure design, a different phenomenon evolved. Students not only addressed the intended objectives but also became so engaged in the problem that they asked stores, businesses, and churches to donate the food goods on their menus. They then arranged to collect the donated food items, contacted the local homeless shelter with donations, and helped to prepare and serve the meal on Thanksgiving Day.

This PBL problem, while intended to be a classroom activity to address curricular objectives, turned into a service learning lesson with a powerful outcome for students and the community. The curriculum objectives were met, and students extended that learning far beyond the classroom. They were immensely proud of what they accomplished, and it had much more meaning for them than if it had been an assigned task.

Other PBL problems are designed with service contributions in mind and are used to increase students' awareness of how others contribute to them and how they can contribute to others while still addressing curricular objectives. This begins in the very early grades with a PBL problem that asks students to consider who keeps their school safe and in good working order besides their teacher. Children as young as 5 years of age will observe that housekeepers, cafeteria workers, and crossing guards are essential to school operation even though they rarely if ever come into the classroom. In this particular problem, students are then asked to consider ways to recognize these people and the contribution they make. This concept can then be transferred to a broader scope of community at a later development stage. Middle and high school students engage PBL problems aligned with service learning such as the previous Thanksgiving meal problem, a problem that has them find meaningful ways to contribute to the patients at a local comprehensive cancer center while learning about the disease and how chemotherapy works to treat it, and in a problem that has them design a more humane animal shelter to replace an existing one within the county budget for improvements.

There is plenty of evidence that when students are more engaged in their learning activities, they learn more and feel more rewarded by what they learn. PBL and service learning provide powerful opportunities for students to do both simultaneously.

PBL and Project-Based Learning

Project-based learning is often referred to as PBL, but to avoid confusion in this section, it will be referred to simply as *project learning*. There is also a distinction to be made between project learning as a strategy and projects that are aligned with classroom instruction as an activity or end product. Those types of projects usually represent something that the student has learned through a course of study and may be considered a performance evaluation.

Project learning, on the other hand, is a strategy that produces new knowledge and is interdisciplinary by design. The method is a comprehensive approach to instruction to foster the use of a variety of skills. Project learning is inclusive of collaboration, problem solving, knowledge construction, and self-evaluation. It also allows students to have more choice in creating their own assignments within the project. The intention is to give students a sense of ownership and control over their learning.

An example of project learning from the Buck Institute for Education (Thomas, 2002) follows:

> In a middle school Biology course, students experiment with protists (one-celled organisms like algae and bacteria). The goal of the project is to develop a new food product. Students grow a variety of protist cultures, evaluate existing food products containing protists (e.g., yogurt, yeast), gather data on various growth factors, experiment with a number of potential food products, and develop a marketing plan for a new product.

Students must do their own exploration of these central concepts to determine how they will proceed with the project. They work in small groups on the project and design their own learning needs.

The elements in project learning that directly align with PBL are numerous. Students work in small groups to develop their own learning objectives in order to solve the problem they have been given. They must acquire new content in a variety of subject areas and be able to apply what they learn in this example by developing a new food product and designing a marketing plan.

Now consider integrating this lesson plan with the PBL strategy. Much of the project learning example would remain the same. However, students would be given a role in the problem to make it even more real to them. In this example, students might be placed in the role of head of the research and development department for Mega Foods. They would be provided examples of other foods produced by Mega Foods, perhaps even some of their latest developments. It would be consistent with the PBL methodology to make these foods attractive to middle school students. For example, students might be told in the PBL scenario that Mega Foods produces mainly snacks or fast foods. Now the project learning has been placed in a context that gives it even more meaning for the students. It is important to consistently demonstrate for middle and high school students where the content they explore actually shows up in the real world around them. The project learning activities in this example are greatly enhanced by having students better understand how they or others might use the information they learn later in life.

It is also important to remember that middle and high school students are in a developmental stage where career considerations are a real part of their thinking. The roles given to students in PBL problems foster the opportunity to increase their awareness of career opportunities and to further explore what people in certain occupations actually do in their jobs. In existing PBL scenarios, students must determine what genetics counselors, highway engineers, triage nurses, landscape architects, and city planners do in their jobs every day.

PBL provides a context for strategies such as project learning to broaden the scope of what students learn and its meaningfulness to them.

PBL and Traditional Strategies

The nontraditional design of PBL often gives the impression that the more traditional strategies have been or should be abandoned. This is not the intention of PBL. Rather, it is the intention to better use some of the more traditional strategies within the context of PBL to enhance their effectiveness.

Lectures are a good example of a traditional strategy that can be very effective in the appropriate context. The advantage of lectures is that they are an efficient way to deliver expert content to nonexperts. The reality, however, is that lectures are typically rather boring and passive for the learner. Few of us choose to seek out experts and have 50 minutes of uninterrupted talk provided from them in order to learn a new concept. Typically, we prefer to engage in a conversation with the experts and hear from them in smaller packets of their expertise. While this is not always practical with a large group of learners in a traditional classroom setting, it is quite doable in the context of PBL. Lectures can be provided at strategic points within PBL problems to help students move forward with their exploration of new concepts. It is suggested, however, that lectures be retooled so that they do not exceed approximately 10 minutes in length. Lectures that exceed 10 minutes typically derail students from self-directed learning activities that are essential to the effectiveness of PBL. Yet, in these small increments, they are excellent tools for helping students through the complexities of some learning objectives.

Recall the problem of the deformed frogs given in the earlier section on cooperative learning. Over the course of this problem, it might be quite helpful to present the students with several very brief lectures specific to their learning issues. One example might be how toxins in the environment affect development and at what stages this can happen. Another might be on why a certain toxin would be harmful to a frog's development but not to a human's.

A brief lecture is always appropriate when students express frustration or seem stuck in their understanding of a new concept. Be mindful to keep the lectures succinct and be certain that they specifically address a learning issue identified by students.

Other traditional strategies that teachers prefer not to abandon include the use of worksheets for skill practice and handouts for disseminating information more concisely than textbooks. Neither of these strategies needs to be discarded during the use of PBL. But they should be reframed in order to remain consistent with the elements of PBL and to be as effective as possible to promote self-directed learning and higher-order thinking skills.

Worksheets can easily be integrated into the context of a PBL problem in a variety of ways. One example is in the problem called *Fence Me In* provided in Resource A. Students use worksheets to practice determining perimeters and areas as part of this problem for designing fenced areas on a ranch. Another example is in *Teresa and Carl* in Chapter 2. Students use worksheets to help them understand the probabilities that children will inherit particular phenotypes and genotypes based on their parents' genetic profile. They practice using various traits in the Pundett Square worksheets to familiarize themselves with these concepts. They can then more easily consider the traits and their dominance or recessiveness in the case of *Teresa and Carl.*

Handouts are also very useful in PBL lessons but are distributed differently than in traditional lesson plans. In many cases, teachers have developed handouts to convey information to students in a clearer way than a textbook or other source might provide. In PBL, it is suggested that handouts be renamed resources and distributed to students or student groups when their content shows up on the learning issues list. For example, in the service learning scenario about planning a menu for Thanksgiving Day, students might be provided a handout with the daily nutritional requirements for adults and children. Once students list the need to know this information, the teacher might provide them with a resource, the handout, in order to move them forward in their learning in this and other areas. If the teacher deems it is more valuable for students to have this information quickly rather than to look it up, then distributing the handout is an effective way to get the information to them. It is important to remember that, as with lectures, the use of handouts as a way to distribute resource information is much more effective if the students have asked for the information. Distributing handouts or delivering lectures before the students express the need undermines the principle of having the students identify their own learning needs. Teachers may find it difficult or uncomfortable to wait, but patience usually pays off if the problem is well constructed and the facilitation prompts students to recognize the need for the handout or lecture content.

Using It All, Using It Well

Carol Ann Tomlinson (2002) reminds us, "Students care deeply about learning when their teachers meet their need for affirmation, contribution, purpose, power, and challenge." Clearly, there are many strategies available to do these things that invite students to learn. However, access to the understanding of these strategies and how to integrate them into effective classroom practice often leaves teachers with the impression that each approach is somehow exclusive of the other. To the contrary, the complementary nature of most of the newer strategies and of the more traditional strategies is likely to be the most powerful strategy of all.

The constant challenge for teachers is one of student engagement. Even the most novice teacher recognizes that once a student is hooked, they are at an optimal place for learning to take place. Most of the strategies discussed in this chapter are designed to help create that hook in students, to engage them in their own learning in powerful ways. Other strategies are effective in meeting the learning needs once the hook has occurred. The key for teachers is in finding the balance of what is available to promote learning and self-direction in students.

PBL provides a context for the use of the most innovative approaches and for the tried and true methods that teachers have acquired through years of experience.

7

PBL Beyond the Middle and High School Classrooms

I may have said the same thing before . . . but my explanation,
I am sure, will always be different.

—Oscar Wilde

The Future for Students

Each fall, thousands of recent high school graduates head off to a 2- or 4-year college or to the world of work. They are excited about the prospects that lie ahead; they are proud to have been selected for the incoming class of freshmen or selected for their new job. Unfortunately, for more and more high school graduates, some of the most critical tools they will need for future success are ones that may not have been provided in traditional classrooms. These students will, sadly, find themselves unprepared for the rigor of college courses, the expectations of employers, and the need to self-direct a significant portion of the lifelong learning that lies ahead of them.

Recall from the Preface that about 75% of today's high school graduates will go to college within 2 years of graduation. The fact that high school students are increasingly unprepared for college work is not a reflection that students are less smart than they used to be or that they simply do not work hard enough once they get to college. It is much more likely a result of curricula throughout their K-12 experiences that over-emphasize rote memorization and content recall in the absence of a meaningful context. The standard course of study rarely focuses on developing problem-solving skills, self-directed learning strategies, or inquiry to acquire content to the same extent that it focuses on recitation and item recognition for multiple choice testing.

The rigor, accountability, and independent elements of college course work are a rude awakening for students who are accustomed to being provided handouts with the information needed to pass an examination, instructed chapter and verse where to access information, and are so teacher directed that they are at a loss about what to do unless given a specific assignment.

Likewise, most employment situations will place demands on students to be critical thinkers, to self-direct some of their learning process on the job, and to be problem solvers. In their article titled "Skills Employers Seek," Lloyd and Kennedy (1997) list the eight most desired characteristics as identified by potential employers. The list below represents the order and a brief description from that list.

It is evident from this list and many similar ones that employers value a skill set that is quite distinct from the ability to memorize facts and recognize information. In order for students to be well prepared for the challenges that await them in the employment sector, they must have some opportunity to practice these skills and this type of skill development. PBL is an excellent mechanism for students to develop and to refine these abilities and aptitudes. In the PBL context, there is also a relevance and value given to the use of these skills and to acquiring a high level of competence in each of them.

Similarly, PBL provides a strong foundation for the rigors of college work that will be expected of students. Through consistent use of PBL for new learning, students learn how to learn, what to learn, and how to find what they need to learn. They become less

---

Box 7.1 Skills Employers Seek

Adaptability. Develop a habit of curiosity, think creatively, solve problems quickly and effectively, and work well with those different from you.

Competences in Reading and Writing. Extract important ideas from written words, apply information to solve problems, and communicate (orally) clearly, accurately, and logically.

Communication Skills. Be curious enough to probe for critical information, be able to determine that you and another have a common understanding, communicate ideas concisely and persuasively.

Computer Skills. Be able to use the Internet, be able to use a word processing program, be able to use a database management program.

Group Interactional Skills. Solve problems in a group, judge and engage in appropriate behavior, cope with undesirable behavior in others, share responsibility with others, negotiate, and deal with ambiguity.

Interpersonal Influence Skills. Achieve personal goals and influence others, understand organizational structure, understand decision-making processes.

Knowing How to Learn. Understand how to absorb and retain information, learn when to learn, stay aware of external events and their influence.

Self-Management Skills. Believe in self-worth, take responsibility, generate internal motivation, take actions that ensure personal and career development.

---

dependent on handouts and more familiar with researching for themselves. Students become less dependent on direction from the teacher and more confident in their own self-direction abilities. In essence, students become better prepared for a college learning lifestyle where less is provided for them in terms of directives and more is expected from them in terms of initiative. Whether a student is entering a college or university immersed in PBL instruction or a more traditional institution, a PBL background will have better prepared that student for what lies ahead.

PBL fosters self-directed learning, independent and interdependent research, inquiry, hypotheses generation, discernment of credible sources and resources, new information acquisition, hypotheses testing, hypotheses revision, and confident decision making. Other benefits include increased communication skills, integration of technology and instruction, higher retention of learned content, integrating and synthesizing new content, applying new content to appropriate situations, and accurately self-assessing to determine knowledge gaps. These are the characteristics and attributes that serve all learners in both formal and informal learning situations. Why not start to sponsor this kind of development in middle school students and continue it throughout the formal educational experiences of all students? Doing so will better prepare students for a college career, workforce entry, and their lifelong learning pursuits.

The Future for PBL

Educators and education experts have explored many trends in attempts to improve student performance, enhance teaching strategies, and better prepare graduating students for their next set of challenges. So many trends have been explored, it seems, that teachers often refer to them as "the flavor of the month." Sustainability of such trends is often not evident, and teachers typically return to their own comfortable style once they have tried out a new practice. This appears not to be the case with PBL teachers, and for good reasons.

Teachers report that in addition to the many student benefits of PBL, there are numerous teacher benefits. PBL teachers experience the fundamental elements of teaching that first attracted them to the profession. They interact more with their students; they share the joy of discovery with their students; they share the pride of accomplishment with their students.

Teachers say they feel they are making a greater impact on students' lives by giving them the skills to learn on their own. Most teachers came to the profession hoping to influence and impact their students' lives in meaningful ways. They feel that PBL provides more and better chances to do this. And at the end of the day, teachers say it is both more fun and more effective to teach and learn using PBL.

This helps explain the sustainability of PBL, and that explains why its use is becoming more widespread. While medical schools are credited with being the birthplace of PBL, its prevalence has grown to include other professional graduate schools, 4-year universities, community colleges, and many K-12 school systems.

Today, all 125 medical schools in the United States report a PBL component within their curriculum. Others report a full transition to a PBL course of study. Likewise, most veterinary schools report the use of PBL throughout the curriculum. At Samford University in Birmingham, Alabama, the Center for Problem-Based Learning recently developed a list of under-graduate institutions that shows that 74 universities self-report that they offer PBL courses. Of those 74, at least 16 have extensive outreach programs to K-12 school systems. It is likely that this number underrepresents the current level of activity in PBL initiatives. Whatever the true number currently is, the evidence is that the practice of PBL continues to grow and is being sustained.

Community colleges have demonstrated a significant increase in the use of PBL over the last 10 years as the result of a major initiative, the Curriculum Improvement Project, or CIP. In North Carolina alone, a recent PBL Conference for Community College Faculty resulted in 93 participants representing 70% of the community colleges in the state system.

The use of PBL has grown well beyond the standard of a "trend." Rather, PBL, as a methodology to address many of the educational concerns and criticisms, is becoming a preva-lent practice. For instance, Southern Illinois University School of Medicine has reported rapid dissemination within School District 186 in Springfield, Illinois. It was further reported that teachers there perceive PBL as the solution to many problems in K-12 education.

PBL addresses many concerns one sees daily in the media as well as professional journals. Problems include disinterested students, poor scores on standardized national examinations, low retention of learned material, inability to apply previously learned information, and low evidence of critical and higher order thinking skills. In the information-driven and technology-oriented society we have today, and will have in the future, there is significant concern over these issues. PBL addresses these deficiencies and does so in the absence of rote, mundane "skill-and-drill" exercises. Instead, PBL gives meaning to the learning that takes place. It gives a relevancy to the information that supports its retention and transferability to different situations. Additionally, as more and more postsecondary institutions incorporate PBL practices, students' successful preparation must begin during their K-12 experiences. For students who move directly into employment after high school graduation, the advantages from PBL experiences will much better serve them in the world of work.

The good news is that the use of PBL does not require classroom teachers to abandon the strategies and approaches that have worked well for them. PBL gives these practices a context that makes them more meaningful and more effective. Teachers have already acknowledged the value of collaborative learning, problem-solving exercises, and independent study. PBL provides a framework that integrates these successful strategies and, at the same time, puts excitement back into learning.

This book is not meant to give the impression that PBL can and will fix all the ills in the current educational system. It is intended, however, that teachers find here a useful and meaningful strategy to increase student learning that complements many of the things they are already successfully doing. The hope is that teachers will find as many benefits for themselves as for their students. Teachers have always been the source of dedication, inspiration, and enthusiasm that creates the momentum necessary to make meaningful changes in classroom practices. The true merit of this book is, perhaps, in providing the spark that feeds the passion and perseverance of classroom teachers.

Educators must hold a vision for the future that includes preparing students in the best possible ways for postsecondary experiences, whether in higher education or work. That foundation, in order to meet the demands of today's and tomorrow's society, will prepare students with an extensive, integrated knowledge base that is effectively retained and easily recalled. It will give students the necessary skills to acquire information on their own and apply it in problem-solving situations. Students will be prepared to be effective collaborators with peers and supervisors. And perhaps most important, students will have developed the self-directed learning skills to be effective, independent learners for the rest of their lives.

Resource A

Additional PBL Problems for
Middle School and High School

Middle School PBL Problems

A Thought for Your Penny

You work in research and development at the U.S. Mint. You are assigned to design a new penny for the future. It must be tarnish proof and maintain the same size/mass as a standard penny.

What do you already know about size and mass of pennies?
Are there rules or regulations about what can be put on the design of a coin?
What makes something tarnish proof?

The objectives for this problem include mass, weight, properties of metals, alloys, design, cost of metals, and communication skills. There are many existing, effective labs on matter that teachers should feel free to bring into this problem. Flame testing and electroplating activities are two suggestions.

Another suggestion to effectively embed the communication objectives is to have the students write a letter to the U.S. Mint that includes their new penny design and explains its merits.

Let's Go to the Fair

Scenario 1: You are a design engineer at Fun Time Designs. Mr. Newton, president and owner of the Fair Days Amusement Park, is in need of some engineering expertise to restore the park. He wishes to restore the original Newtonian Adventure Themes section of the park. (Mr. Newton is the descendant of a very famous scientist, and he would like the park to reflect as many of his ancestor's discoveries as possible.) Some of the rides are in excellent shape, while others need repair and replacement. Mr. Newton's immediate concern is to get new designs for the rides that are not operational and not repairable.

The first ride that Mr. Newton wants to build is the vertical fall ride. This ride must meet the following criteria: (a) actual ride should fall between 8.0 and 10.0 meters and (b) figures for acceleration at ground zero should be calculated. The design of all rides should include mechanical drawings, should be tested and retested, and should meet all safety requirements before being built and open to the public. Scale models and demonstrations of each ride are required.

Who is Mr. Newton's ancestor?
What kinds of discoveries did he make?
How will this affect your designs for rides in the park?

This problem has multiple scenarios to keep the students engaged in the intended learning areas.

Scenario 2: Because of Fun Time Designs' success with the vertical fall ride, Mr. Newton has asked that you design a ride that (a) is not powered by gravity or a motor, (b) needs to accelerate from a resting position, (c) is not limited to ground travel, and (d) must travel horizontally for a period of time. The model to be demonstrated to Mr. Newton should be able to travel a minimum of 1.5 meters and a maximum of 3.0 meters, and remain within a width of 1.0 meter.

Scenario 3: Mr. Newton has now asked Fun Time Designs to create a third ride for his amusement park completely different from the other two rides. This ride is (a) to be powered by gravity, (b) to be self-stopping, and (c) to travel horizontally part of the time. The model of the ride should run at least 4.0 meters and no more than 5.0 meters in length, and remain within a width of 1.0 meter.

The use of all three scenarios comprises an eighth grade physics unit. This unit typically lasts for about 3 weeks. The learning objectives include understanding gravitational forces, friction and motion relationships, Newton's Laws, measurement, indirect proportion, and simple machines.

Amphibian Anxiety

You are a camp counselor at Camp Malf. The camp director has received a letter from a concerned parent, whose child came home from camp and described deformed frogs in the area where camp activities were taking place. The parent wants to know if frogs in the area are indeed deformed, and, if so, are the children at any risk.

(Continued)

(Continued)

Mr. Dewey, the camp director, has asked you and the other counselors to advise him on an appropriate response. Mr. Dewey wants you to study the frog deformation problem and determine if there is a potential hazard to the campers. You may wish to gather data as well as interpret data collected from area scientists. You will be reporting your findings regularly.

What do you think the parent means by "deformed"?
What else would be helpful to know to start your investigation?

This problem comes with a map of the area that shows a lake and the adjoining camp property. The map shows the location of other nearby properties such as an abandoned air base, a housing development, a Christmas tree farm, and agricultural land growing apples and tobacco. The primary learning objective is to develop an understanding of human and environmental interaction. Students typically research factors in the development of amphibians as well.

Grow Veggies Grow

You have just graduated from State University and have purchased a small 10-acre farm in the Piedmont region of North Carolina. With a degree in agriculture, you have decided to pursue organic farming. You will need to develop a 5-year plan and decide what crops you want to grow and sell.

What do you know?
What additional information do you need to begin to develop your plan?

Students are expected to raise learning issues about organic farming, crop rotation, soil quality, weather conditions, use of pesticides, use of fertilizers, and weed control. Two science lab activities accompany this problem. One has students make their own soil, while the other has them compare and contrast different soil samples. Students are provided with several Internet resources and with paper resources on organic farming once this appears as a learning need on their Learning Issues list. After students have determined the crops they will grow and have designed at least part of their 5-year plan, they are informed through an additional problem scenario that they have an infestation that will have to be controlled. The type of infestation differs from group to group and is distributed by the teacher on a note card to each group. This information is intended to drive students deeper into the exploration of pesticides and insecticides and their impact on plant growth, safety for human consumption, and relationship to what constitutes organic production.

Moonball

You have been elected commissioner of the newly formed Moon Basketball Association. As you establish league play at the recently created moon base station, what changes will you make to the game of basketball for the MBA? You will need to prepare a written justification for any rule changes based on scientific explanations that require the game to be played differently than it is on Earth.

What do you know?
What additional information do you need to determine if rule changes are necessary and what they will be?

In this problem, students are expected to explore issues of gravitational force, weight versus gravity, math conversions, and report writing. An additional scenario to this problem expands the Learning Issues list to include understanding the atmospheric conditions of all the planets. The second scenario is as follows.

> You have now been asked to consider expanding the
> league to an intergalactic league. Prepare an additional
> report on the locations you would consider and if rule
> changes are required for these locations.

Students are given a worksheet to practice weight conversions
for three additional planets and the moon. After researching the
atmospheric conditions of the remaining planets, they can use the
worksheet format for making similar conversions. An assessment
rubric for this problem is provided in Chapter 5.

The next problem, *Getting Decked,* is used in one of the
assessment examples in Chapter 5.

Getting Decked

You have volunteered to work on a Habitat for Humanity
building project. You have been given the responsibility of
completing a purchase requisition for an 8' × 10' foot deck
that will be built on the back of the new home.

What facts do you have?
What additional information would you like to have?
How will you proceed?

Once students have listed their Facts and their Need to Know/
Learning Issues, they are given the second scenario to the problem.

The site forewoman gives you the building specifications
and materials price list to calculate your needs. As she is
about to leave, she tells you that the total cost of the deck
must not exceed $500.

Students are expected to address curriculum objectives of budgeting, precise measurement, estimating, inductive and deductive reasoning concepts, and problem solving. They are given diagrams of the deck by specifications and a list of building materials with corresponding prices per unit. They are given a purchase requisition to complete and accurately reflect their budget.

One of the most comprehensive middle school problems and one that students enjoy a great deal is called *The Southeast Caper*. It is presented in multiple scenarios and covers multiple subject areas.

The Southeast Caper

You are a detective with the county sheriff's department. You have been called to your first murder crime scene. You are told to investigate the scene and to interview one witness, Russell MacIntyre. You are to submit a map of the crime scene and gather notes based on your observations at the scene of the crime.

For this problem, a crime scene is actually created with an outlined body, evidence in the area to be collected, unknown substances and fibers in the area, and there is a person available to interview as a witness. The students discover a large earring, paper knife, cigarette butt, ketchup, lipstick tube, plastic bag with white powder, and an overturned chair. They are expected to record their observations, make measurements, appropriately interview the provided witness but not engage anyone else in conversation during their investigation.

The witness is an employee of the school where the murder has occurred and provides lots of information about potential suspects. For the purposes of problem execution, if a person is unavailable to interview, then the witness statement is provided as a resource. If a person is available to play the witness role, he or she is given the statement information beforehand as a script for how to answer questions. Students are given guidelines on how to conduct an interview when that need to know shows up on their Learning Issues list before they head off to the crime scene.

Students are provided with multiple additional resources and activities throughout this problem. They receive suspect profiles, perform labs on the unknown substances, do fingerprint analysis, write a news release, and re-create elements of the crime event by making predictions about where the murderer was and where the victim was using the measurements and object placements found at the scene. Some classes make a field trip to the local morgue, and others have been visited in the classroom by the medical examiner, a local newspaper reporter, and a local detective.

It is apparent that the Learning Issues list for this problem can be quite extensive. Teachers are reminded that they can always narrow or broaden the Learning Issues list with their facilitation of the problem. This problem was developed by a team of teachers from three different subject areas—science, math, and language arts—and so was intended to have a very broad list of Learning Issues.

The last problem example, *Radon in the House,* is a much more focused problem and is provided as a contrast to the previous problem. The reminder to teachers is that PBL problems can occur over a lengthy number of class periods or for a much shorter period.

Radon in the House

You and your spouse are looking for a new house. The realtor informs you that a house you recently visited and plan to place a bid on has abnormal levels of radon present. You and your spouse must now decide whether to still consider the house for purchase, how you address the problem of radon if you do purchase, and how confident you are that the problem would not resurface if you do purchase.

What do you know from the problem statement?
What additional information would you like to have?
What questions might you ask the realtor or current owners?
What kind of information can you look up or research that would be helpful to you in deciding your next step?

Students are expected to explore what radon is and any related health risks from exposure. They will determine why radon is present in one house and not another, how it is detected, how high levels are corrected/addressed, and if there are implications for the water supply. This problem has resource materials about radon and testing for it that students receive on request. There are also worksheets on radioactivity, half-life disintegrations, and radiation exposure in daily life routines. Students typically get quite engaged with this problem and want to test their own home. Again, it is the real-world nature of the problem that appeals to them.

High School PBL Problems

Many high school PBL problems tend to be more course oriented and focused than do problems at other grade levels. This is mostly a reflection of the course-oriented schedule at the high school level. PBL is not any less effective in this format but may be less interdisciplinary, as PBL problems are written to align with very specific course objectives. Here are some examples.

This problem is aligned with curriculum standards in Algebra I and Geometry.

The Town Square

You are a civil engineer and you have been asked to construct roads in a rural area of Montana that has no paved roads.

There are four small towns in this area that are located in a perfect square relative to each other. Each of the towns wishes to be connected directly or indirectly to the others by a paved road. The towns are rural and function on a very small budget. Therefore, the four towns must be connected utilizing the least amount of pavement.

What do you know from the problem statement?
What additional information would you like to have?
How will you proceed?

Students are expected to work with 30/60-degree triangles, solve equations with one unknown, use square roots, solve for the perimeter of a square, and use the Pythagorean theorem. Each student group is asked to submit two plans for consideration by the town councils, along with their justification for use of either plan. Additional scenarios include a mailed diagram of the area with dimensions and distances (that are usually asked for by students) and for preliminary work before traveling to Montana, and another note with costs of some of the possible venues.

Fence Me In

You have just declared your major in college at the end of your sophomore year, and you have decided to be an agricultural engineer. You and three classmates have been hired as part of your program to work on a ranch in Montana for one month.

Upon arriving at the ranch, your first duty is to design the fencing around the rancher's grazing land for sheep, cattle, and horses. Your objective is to use the least amount of fencing possible.

What do you know from the problem statement?
What additional information would you like to have?
How will you proceed?

In this prealgebra problem, students are expected to solve a problem that relates geometric concepts to a real-world situation, use application of measurement, select an appropriate unit tool to find measurement, use calculators, and use exponentiation. Students subsequently learn that the rancher has 275 acres of land and wants 225 acres fenced. Sheep will need one third of the acreage, cattle will need two fifths, and the remainder is for the horses. A scale map is provided of the land depicting a house, barn, and wooded area that should remain as is and that shows a broad stream cutting across the property. The rancher reminds students to consider the needs of each group of animals as their area is designed.

Although students will do some additional research on the animals' needs, they will spend the majority of their learning time in the math requirements of this problem.

The next two problem examples are aligned with the high school science curriculum. The first is a Biology PBL problem and is referenced in Chapter 5 in the assessment examples.

Lost Without a Cell Phone

You are the member of a camera crew for an award-winning film company. You are doing a documentary on the human body and have been miniaturized and injected into a human body to film. However, you quickly find yourself trapped inside the nucleus of a pancreas cell when your micro-vehicle malfunctions. You have no way of communicating with anyone on the outside to tell them where you are or to get help. Without a propulsion system, you need to find your way out of the cell safely.

What do you know from the problem statement?
What additional information would you like to have?
How will you proceed?

Students are first facilitated to describe what they can see in the environment they are in and to describe how it seems to be functioning. They must then make a plan for getting out of the nucleus. The intended objectives are to gain knowledge of (a) cell structures, including the nucleus, cytoplasm, organelles, and the cell membrane, (b) cell functions, including membrane transport, DNA replication, protein synthesis, and mitosis, and (c) the interdependence of cell structures and functions. Students must first find their way out of the nucleus and then out of the cell in order to resolve this problem. In the process, they will explore the structure and function of the pancreas, what it secretes, and how its cells work. Students typically do a lot of diagramming with this problem and sometimes construct three-dimensional models to demonstrate their resolutions.

Another science-related problem is specific to understanding three-dimensional anatomy. The problem is called *The Latter-Day Robin Hood* and is also included in assessment examples in Chapter 5.

The Latter-Day Robin Hood

You are the doctor on duty in the emergency room one Saturday night when you are asked to speak on the phone with a badly shaken caller. The phone connection is poor and transmission is garbled, but you believe you hear "We'll be there in about 20 minutes. My buddy is doin' real bad. We were out in the mountains . . . He . . . [static] . . . He's real pale, shocky, maybe . . . sleepy . . ."

Ten minutes later, another caller is on the phone asking for you. He tells you that he is a member of a survivalist group that was practicing war games in a wilderness area near Pilot Mountain. One of the party, after a bit of drinking, accidentally wounded another with a metal-tipped hunting arrow from point-blank range. After the injury occurred, he left the group to find a land-line phone while the others left for the hospital.

When you ask, "How bad was the wound?" the caller blurts out, "Shot clean through!" You ask, "Where?" and the caller says, "I'm not really sure, just clean through."

When you ask, "How was your friend doing when you left them?" the caller tells you that his friend was pale and shocky, coughing up blood, vomiting blood, and peeing blood. He should be in the ER in just a few minutes.

What do you know from the problem statement?
What additional information would you like to have?
How will you proceed?

Students are next prompted to prepare for the victim's arrival at the emergency room. They must consider what kind of medical treatment he may need and where the arrow is likely to be embedded. Students must explore anatomy issues, including where the organs are, which organs have likely been struck by the arrow, organ placement when sitting, standing, breathing in, breathing out, and abnormal blood flow. One of the most innovative student approaches was the group that requested a hanging skeleton as a resource. They then blew up different colored balloons, labeled them as organs, and placed them within the skeleton. The students then took a wooden dowel, placed a paper arrow tip on it, and tried out various angles to support or rule out different hypotheses. It is a safe bet that these students will always have a frame of reference for where their heart, lungs, kidneys, and stomach are located.

The next problem is an example of a social studies problem, inclusive of objectives in world history, U.S. history, and political science. This problem is also an example of a format that allows the teacher to fill in the blank with the most timely content.

Meddler, Policeman, or Peacekeeper

You are the current secretary of state and you are responsible for briefing, on a daily basis, the president of the United States of the potential troubles in the world that need U.S. action or consideration. Your responsibilities include recommending a course of action to the president.

Today, this is the information in your briefing:

(Here the teacher can insert current events content appropriate for the curriculum objectives. One example follows.)

- There is currently an opportunity to diplomatically overcome U.N. resistance to using force to disarm Iraq. You and the president have been given time on the schedule in 2 days to speak to the U.N.'s Security Council.

(Continued)

(Continued)

- It was reported today by a Pakistani intelligence official that a captured al-Qaeda leader has indicated that Osama bin Laden is alive, in good health, and living in the border region between Pakistan and Afghanistan.

What do you know?
What do you need to know?
How will you proceed?

This problem can be as broad and encompassing or as narrow as the teacher decides. The typical standard course of study objectives that are intended by the problem include analyzing problems and assessing prospects of an interdependent world; assessing the degree to which the international community is capable of resolving recurring global dilemmas; analyzing the causes and effects of U.S. involvement in international affairs; assessing the influence of phenomena such as television on the conduct of American politics; establishing the role of organizations set up to maintain peace and judge their continuing effectiveness; identifying examples of domestic and international economic interdependence; analyzing the relationships between economic conditions and political decisions; identifying key government officials, how they are chosen, and their duties and responsibilities; evaluating the role of debate, consensus, compromise, and negotiation in resolving conflicts; acquiring information from a variety of sources; using acquired information for problem solving and decision making; and analyzing formal and informal means of interacting with the governments of other nations.

This particular problem can obviously be used in a very comprehensive fashion, and even the list of potential objectives provided is not exclusive. Remember, however, that the teacher can determine the breadth of any problem through facilitation. Only one or two of these objectives might be chosen as a focus, and facilitation by the teacher will have the students target those learning areas.

In this next problem that aligns with English, Language Arts, and Literature curricula, the problem focus is more narrow but the range of objectives remains broad. This problem is called *Jazz Up Literature.*

Jazz Up Literature

You are a writer who wishes to submit your writing for a book on modern writers of American literature. You are preparing a chapter on the Harlem Renaissance. The chapter must focus on one author from this period who is worthy of exemplifying the whole period.

What do you know?
What do you need to know?
How will you proceed?

The next scenario provides criteria for the students to use and anticipates the type of the information they will have identified in their Need to Know list.

You are competing for this chapter submission with 15 other authors. The editor has determined that points will be awarded for meeting the following criteria:
Your chapter must include

1. How your selected author illustrates themes of the Harlem Renaissance through one of his or her works (30 points)

2. Background information on your author relevant to theme (10 points)

3. Careful literary analysis, comparison, and discussion of your writer and your selection of his or her work (30 points)

(Continued)

(Continued)

4. A dramatization of the selected work from memory and presentation of segments from #1, #2, and #3 above (30 points)

What do you need to know now?
How will you narrow your focus? What will your focus be?
How will you proceed?

Students are then asked by the editor to submit a draft of their chapter, and a checklist is provided to guide them in its preparation. After the drafts are completed, students receive an additional scenario where they have been asked to participate in a peer review of submitted chapters. Now student groups review each other's work, using the checklists of criteria to critique their chapter drafts. They must prepare a written critique of their peers' work using a specified format.

Intended objectives in this problem include defending argumentative positions on literary issues; critically interpreting and evaluating experiences, literature, language, and ideas; demonstrating an understanding of selected world literature through interpretation and analysis; selecting and exploring works that relate to an issue, author, or theme of world literature; and documenting the reading of student-chosen works.

The participation of the students in the peer critique process not only broadens the objectives to be met but also alleviates some of the time demand placed on teachers to perform this kind of review. Teachers can review the critiques for accuracy and thoroughness by having one group present their critiques of another group's work and facilitating the response or defense of the source group. This furthers the objectives again by addressing oral communication as well as written communication learning issues.

In this last high school problem example, *Snap, Crackle, Pop,* there is slightly more integration of subject matter. The intended focus is on oral and written communications, but students must draw on existing content or acquire new content to fully resolve the problem.

Snap, Crackle, Pop

Your company has just developed a new breakfast cereal. Your department, marketing and advertising, is expected to present an advertisement campaign for this new cereal to the president of the company in 2 weeks. This presentation will need to include a product name, packaging, marketing strategies, and target consumers.

What do you know?
What do you need to know?
How will you proceed?

In subsequent scenarios, students learn additional facts, such as the cereal is not presweetened, they must provide a packaging prototype for the cereal box, they must have a slogan and a jingle at the presentation, and at least three marketing strategies are to be presented. They also receive a notice regarding the federal law that prohibits making knowingly false statements about a product.

The objectives is this problem include creating an effective response to the task in form, content, and language; demonstrating reflection and insight as well as evidence of analytical, critical, or evaluative thinking; using convincing elaboration and development to clarify an idea; using logical organization for the task; using language appropriate for the intended audience; and giving formal oral presentations with fluency and effectiveness.

Typically, students must familiarize themselves with the usual nutritional content of breakfast cereals, perform some measurements for box design, and even do some volume conversion. This problem is included as an example not only because it covers a range of these standard curriculum objectives but it has historically been one of the most fun problems that students engage. There is opportunity for some students to create the artwork, design the jingle composition, and rehearse performance as the oral presentation is prepared.

Hopefully, the range of problem formats, subject areas, and grade levels in this section have provided a sound level of insight into how PBL problems are effectively used in middle and high school classrooms, how PBL problems are delivered, and how they can be created to best suit your own style and curriculum needs.

Resource B

PBL Process Charts

The following pages are examples of completed PBL process charts. The first example is for the middle school problem *Player's Choice* in Chapter 2. Notice that multiple charts are used for this problem. This problem is intended to extend over multiple days, and multiple scenarios are given to the students. With each new scenario, or each time they acquire new information on their own, the original or previous list must be revisited. The list will be updated to reflect new facts (some that have been researched and some that have been provided in the new scenario), new Need to Know items, new Learning Issues, and possible revisions in the Possible Solutions list. These charts, or something similar, assist the students in documenting their progress, keeping up with their learning issues, and keeping each other accountable for individual contributions to the group's work on the problem. Some teachers require that students turn in one copy of their chart so that the teacher can monitor in a detailed manner their progress, learning issues, and the process being used to determine viable solutions.

The second example is for the high school problem *Read All About It* in Chapter 3. Because this is a more focused problem, only one chart is required for students to document their facts, Need to Know items, Learning Issues, and Possible Solutions. How the charts are used is at the teacher's discretion. The more familiar and experienced teachers become with the PBL process and the variety of problems, the easier it is to determine how using these charts or something of a similar format will support PBL instruction in the classroom.

PBL PROCESS (using multiple charts)

Case Name: Player's Choice, Day 1

Fact List	Need to Know	Learning Issues
Statistician for NBA team Analyze data for 15 players Select five best for starting lineup Make graphic presentation	Statistics on the players: field goals, free throws, steals, turnovers, assists, rebounds, personal fouls, blocks, minutes played	What are averages? How are statistics compiled and who does it? How do you know what statistics represent? How do you make a graphic presentation of information? What is percentage/ratio in statistics?

Possible Solutions	New Learning Issues
Any lineup with five players with stats that can be defended. A lineup with five players who have highest field goals, assisting, and high playing time. A lineup with five players who have high scoring, good rebounding, low number of fouls.	What is unprofessional behavior? Why is drug use a reason for suspension? What happens when stats are rounded up or down? Can we have statistics for more than 1 year?

Defendable Solution(s)
The three possible solutions are still defendable until more research is done.

PBL PROCESS

Case Name: Player's Choice, Day 2

Fact List	Need to Know	Learning Issues
Statistics on players: Games played Games started Minutes played Field goals made Field goals attempted Three-point shots made Three-point shots attempted Free throws made Free throws attempted Offensive rebounds Defensive rebounds Assists Total rebounds made Personal fouls Steals Turnovers Blocks Times fouled out Total points/season	What position did each player have when they earned these stats? Do they play for an NBA team now? When they earned these stats? Did they play in college? Are those stats available? How long have they been playing in the NBA?	Which positions need to be the highest scorers? Which positions need to be the best rebounders? Which positions need to be best at assists? How do coaches make strategies and plays based on using the players' statistics? Does averaging the statistics for 2 different years change who the five best players are?

Possible Solutions	New Learning Issues
Any lineup with five players with stats that can be defended. A lineup with five players who have highest field goals, assisting, and high playing time. A lineup with five players who have high scoring, good rebounding, low number of fouls.	Who will be the coach? What is his record like? How long has he coached? What should a graph include to defend our selected team?

Defendable Solution(s)
Players A, B, D, J, and N.

PBL PROCESS

Case Name: Player's Choice, Day 3

Fact List	Need to Know	Learning Issues
Centers: A = Kareem Abdul-Jabbar C = Wilt Chamberlain E = Alonzo Mourning **Power Forwards:** B = James Worthy F = Dennis Rodman K = Glen Rice **Small Forwards:** D = Julius Erving H = Charles Barkley M = Larry Bird **Shooting Guards:** J = Michael Jordan L = Pete Maravich O = Clyde Drexler **Point Guards:** G = Mugsy Bogues I = John Stockton N = Ervin Johnson	How old is each player on the list? Do any players have old or new injuries that might affect future statistics in any of the areas? Do players get along with each other? Have any been suspended from a team for anything in the past? Have any ever been thrown out of a game?	Compare players' statistics based on number of years played. For example, if stats are for last 2 years, see if those 2 years are the 2nd and 3rd year played or the 6th and 7th year played. Compare the same years for all players to see if stats change a lot.

Defendable Solution(s)
Players A, B, D, J, and N.
Defense is provided in graphic presentation prepared for the team owner.

PBL PROCESS (single-day chart)

Case Name: Read All About It

Fact List	Need to Know	Learning Issues
You are a newspaper editor. You must supervise the preparation of the front page of Sat. newspaper. The front page needs to be more appealing. The most important articles go on the front page. You must approve and select the articles.	Who reads this paper? What does the front page look like now? How experienced is the staff? What is the budget? What types of articles are usually on the front page? How much color can be used?	What makes a good article good and a bad article bad? How long should articles be? How much space is on the front page? Are there studies that show what is appealing about newspapers and what is not appealing? Is there a "best" way to organize a front page?

Possible Solutions	New Learning Issues
Change the types of stories on the front page. Make front page articles longer/shorter. Add more color, different fonts, different font sizes.	Can the layout be done on the computer first? Can the new layout be "tested" with a few people before it is printed?

Defendable Solution(s)
Make the front page more colorful, with more interesting articles. Field test the new design before printing copies to be sold.

Resource C

Guidelines for Facilitating PBL

This section provides general guidelines for facilitating PBL problems and assisting students in their learning through the PBL process. The most fundamental caution is not to be too directive and to keep the learning student centered.

The first list gives suggestions for prompters that keep students moving forward without telling them what they should be doing or taking the problem away from them.

The second list gives reminders of behaviors to avoid that could possibly disrupt a student-centered learning process.

Facilitator Do's

- Do use prompting questions that are open ended, such as
  - What would it be helpful to know now?
  - Is that a learning issue?
  - How do you know that?
  - What does that have to do with the problem?
  - Does everyone agree with that statement?
  - Where are you stuck?
  - Can you agree what the next step should be?
  - Say more about what you are thinking about that.
  - Where can you find that kind of information?
  - Somebody summarize where you are right now.
  - What do you agree to do before you meet about this again?

- Do make brief notes to yourself before intervening.
- Do count to 10 or 20 before intervening.
- Do give students time to self-correct before you do it for them.
- Do be in the problem with the students rather than an observer who knows how it turns out.
- Do be patient and let the students make mistakes. Powerful learning occurs in mistake making.
- Do help students discover how to correct mistakes and avoid the same ones in the future.
- Do get excited with the students and enjoy the learning with them.

Facilitator Don'ts

- Don't take the problem away from the students by being too directive.
- Don't send messages that they are thinking the "wrong" way or doing the "wrong" thing.
- Don't give them too much information because you are afraid they won't find it.
- Don't intervene the moment you sense they are off track—remember, mistakes are okay.
- Don't rush them, especially in the beginning.
- Don't be afraid to say, "That sounds like a learning issue to me" instead of telling them the "answer."
- Don't worry. Students will learn lots of content, become sound critical thinkers, and enjoy PBL lesson days.

References

Delisle, R. (1997). *How to use problem-based learning in the classroom.* Alexandria, VA: Association for Supervision and Curriculum Development.

Haycock, K. (1999). Ticket to nowhere. *Thinking K-16, 3,* 3-31.

Jacobs, G. M., Power, M. A., & Inn, L. W. (2002). *The teacher's sourcebook for cooperative learning.* Thousand Oaks, CA: Corwin.

Johnson, D. W., Johnson, R. T., & Holubec, E. J. (1993). *Cooperation in the classroom* (6th ed.). Edina, MN: Interaction.

Lloyd, M. A., & Kennedy, J. H. (1997). *Skills employers seek.* Retrieved from http://www.psychwww.com/careers/skills.htm.

National Research Council. (1996). *The National Science Education Standards.* Washington, DC: National Academy Press.

Thomas, J. W. (2002). *PBL: An overview of project-based learning.* Retrieved from http://www.bie.org/pbl/.

Tomlinson, C. A. (2002). Invitations to learn. *Educational Leadership, 60*(1), 6-10.

Additional PBL Readings

Barrows, H. (1988). *The tutorial process.* Springfield, IL: Southern Illinois University School of Medicine.

Gallagher, S. A., Sher, B. T., Stepien, W. J., & Workman, D. (1995). Implementing problem-based learning in science classrooms. *School Science and Mathematics, 95*(3), 136-146.

Glasgow, N. A. (1997). *New curriculum for new times: A guide to student-centered, problem-based learning.* Thousand Oaks, CA: Corwin.

Stepien, W. J., Senn, P. R., & Stepien, W. C. (2001). The Internet and problem-based learning: Developing solutions through the Web. Tucson, AZ: Zephyr.

Torp, L. T., & Sage, S. M. (2002). *Problems as possibilities: Problem-based learning for K-16 education* (2nd ed.). Alexandria, VA: Association for Supervision and Curriculum Development.

Index

**CORWIN
PRESS**

The Corwin Press logo—a raven striding across an open book—represents the union of courage and learning. Corwin Press is committed to improving education for all learners by publishing books and other professional development resources for those serving the field of K–12 education. By providing practical, hands-on materials, Corwin Press continues to carry out the promise of its motto: **"Helping Educators Do Their Work Better."**